D1553369

Praise for *Just Faith*

"A relevant, educational, and informative book that breaks down and explores the relationship of Christianity and social justice. *Just Faith: Reclaiming Progressive Christianity* is putting out a rally cry for Christians to invoke the actions of Jesus to activate, organize, and speak up. As a progressive Christian who has worked at the highest level of politics, this book is an instructional manual that challenges me to do more to be a beacon of love and justice. As Guthrie Graves-Fitzsimmons recounts, many movements with heralded leaders have been built on the foundation of faith. There is not a more urgent moment than now for us all join and unite."

—**Deesha Dyer**, former White House Social Secretary during the Obama administration

"Guthrie Graves-Fitzsimmons answers the questions that anyone interested in the current role and relevance of faith in the public square should be asking. *Just Faith* is an honest and compelling examination of where progressive Christianity's strengths and challenges lie. With the landscape of faith in America so sharply divided along sociopolitical lines, *Just Faith* casts encouraging light on how progressive voices can and must be effective in having impact both now and going forward."

—**Rev. Dr. Derrick Harkins**, National Director of Interfaith Outreach for the Democratic National Committee

"Followers of Jesus have always engaged in progressive activism as we live out our faith in the public square. *Just Faith* encourages us to not just remember our bold tradition but to carry the movement forward. I hope you will join me, Guthrie Graves-Fitzsimmons, and the millions of progressive Christians in this prophetic work of social and economic justice. This book will be one of our guides."

—**Rev. Dr. Jacqueline Lewis**, senior minister, Middle Collegiate Church

"I am personally grateful that Guthrie Graves-Fitzsimmons refuses to be silent about the thirty-five million progressive Christians in America whose faith and practice seems to go largely ignored by the media. Progressive Christianity in America is a sleeping giant, and Graves-Fitzsimmons is our press secretary. Consider yourselves warned."

—**Rev. Nadia Bolz-Weber**, New York Times bestselling author of *Shameless, Accidental Saints*, and *Pastrix*

"Guthrie Graves-Fitzsimmons is the nation's leading expert on progressive Christianity as well as one of the movement's greatest champions. Many of us have grown discouraged as the Christian right hijacked our faith. But the time is coming when progressive Christian voices will once again define public debates as they did during the Civil Rights era. In these dark times this book is bound to help you reclaim your voice as a Christian living out Jesus's call to bring liberation to the poor and oppressed."

—**Rev. Jennifer Butler**, CEO, Faith in Public Life

"In *Just Faith: Reclaiming Progressive Christianity*, Guthrie Graves-Fitzsimmons reminds we who consider ourselves progressive Christians that ours is a tradition grounded solidly in the life and teachings of Jesus Christ. While contemporary narratives focus on the voices and political clout of conservative Christians, Graves-Fitzsimmons helps us remember how progressive Christianity has shaped US history and encourages us to boldly reclaim our place in the public square. This is a timely and most-needed book!"

—**Bishop Karen Oliveto**, Mountain Sky Episcopal Area, United Methodist Church

"Progressives of all religious identities can find hope in a revitalized Christian left. While *Just Faith* is Guthrie Graves-Fitzsimmons's own specific story and rooted in his own Christian faith, it offers a helpful vision for people of all faiths who care about social and economic justice."

—**Wajahat Ali**, New York Times contributing op-ed writer and CNN contributor

"Many of us have been in on a secret for years: progressive Christianity is alive and well in America. *Just Faith* doesn't just let readers in on the secret. It helps us contextualize how our unique American experiment has led to the revival of faith-based activism, and it grounds us in the understanding that none of us are alone as progressives within our denominations. Bold, prayerful, and full of knowledge, this is a book to help us find the way."

—**Kaya Oakes**, author of *The Nones Are Alright*

"*Just Faith* is a deeply compelling exploration into the history of how progressive faith has influenced progressive politics in America for the common good. But Guthrie Graves-Fitzsimmons not only explores this often-unknown history, he also shines a light on the growing revival taking place among progressive Christians who are awakening to the Gospel's call to engage in the social and political realities of our world. In an era where the predominant narrative is that progressive faith is dying, *Just Faith* presents a powerful counter-argument that indicates that the future of progressive Christianity is increasingly bright."

—**Rev. Brandan Robertson**, lead pastor of Missiongathering Christian Church and author of *True Inclusion: Creating Communities of Radical Embrace*

JUST FAITH

JUST FAITH

Reclaiming Progressive Christianity

Guthrie Graves-Fitzsimmons

Broadleaf Books

Minneapolis

JUST FAITH
Reclaiming Progressive Christianity

Copyright © 2020 Guthrie Graves-Fitzsimmons. Printed by Broadleaf Books, an imprint of 1517 Media. All rights reserved. Except for brief quotations in critical articles or reviews, no part of this book may be reproduced in any manner without prior written permission from the publisher. Email copyright@1517.media or write to Permissions, Broadleaf Books, PO Box 1209, Minneapolis, MN 55440-1209.

Scripture quotations are from the New Revised Standard Version Bible, copyright © 1989 the Division of Christian Education of the National Council of the Churches of Christ in the United States of America. Used by permission. All rights reserved.

Cover design by Emily Weigel

Print ISBN: 978-1-5064-6252-3
eBook ISBN: 978-1-5064-6253-0

For my grandmother Frances Bell Graves,
who acted justly, loved mercifully,
and walked humbly with God all her days;
who died while I wrote this book;
and whose spirit has an abiding impact on every word.

TABLE OF CONTENTS

TABLE OF CONTENTS

INTRODUCTION

This book began in a foggy haze on the morning of November 9, 2016. Donald Trump's election as president of the United States made many of us despondent about the state of our nation. The general hopelessness for what a Trump administration would bring was coupled with an acute terror at what this meant for religion and politics.

The Democratic Party lost much more than the election. The party also lost the public debate about the "Christian vote" in 2016. Sadly, this wasn't nearly as surprising as the election result itself. The "Christian vote" going for the Republican Party squared neatly with our cultural understanding of faith and politics. It's been talked about that way since before I was born in 1989. A thrice-married real estate developer, who bragged about sexual assault, kept the tradition going. It certainly surprised some political pundits, but for me it deepened how distorted our outlook on Christianity and politics is today.

Christians, we are told, only care about denying women reproductive health care and denying the dignity of LGBTQ people.

This conservative form of Christianity is certainly one version of the faith. It gives the rest of us good reason to believe works of fiction like *The Handmaid's Tale* are close to becoming reality. And conservative Christians have been remarkably successful in capturing our public imagination of Christianity at-large.

My concern about the success of conservative Christianity is that it looks nothing like following Jesus, the teacher and healer who proclaimed a radical vision of the Reign of God coming to earth and who was executed by the state for threatening the status quo.

Since you've picked up this book, I want to honor your time and integrity and let you know up front that I'm a progressive Christian—born, raised, and unapologetic. I recently married my husband, a Presbyterian pastor and therapist, and we believe fully that our marriage is holy and right before God. I stand with Planned Parenthood and teach Bible study classes every Sunday at my Baptist church in Louisville. I believe the Bible calls us to unequivocally support racial justice and guaranteed health care for all as a human right, two ideas affirmed by my seminary education in Christian social ethics. I'm at peace internally about my progressive politics and identity as a follower of Jesus. And throughout these pages, you'll read snippets of my own personal experiences. But my story only represents a part of the larger story of progressive Christianity.

I love the church. I love the church so much that I don't want to look away or diminish its historic and ongoing faults. Growing up in a Methodist church taught me to love my neighbor, work for social justice, and be a part of building the kin-dom* of God. It's because I love the church so dearly that I want to see the movement of people following Jesus live up to who we say we are in the world.

The election of 2016 had many of us down. But it was a moment of *anagnorisis*—a Greek term that is the moment in a story when the main character recognizes or identifies their true nature, recognizes another character's true identity, and discovers the true nature of their current situation—which then leads to the resolution of the story. When historians look back at the history of Christianity and politics in the United States, 2016 will hopefully be marked as the turning of the tide. The alliance between the religious right and the Republican Party held strong despite Donald Trump's rampant immorality, but it also shined a light on the nature of their unholy alliance. And it set us on a course toward the resolution of the story, which is the end of conservative Christian dominance over what it means to be a Christian.

The false prophets of conservative Christianity in the United States have lost credibility as an authentic expression of following Jesus. For many of us, the 2016 election and subsequent actions by President Trump put nails in the coffin of conservative Christianity. Now it's up to us as progressive Christians to drive those

---

* I will use "kin-dom of God" in this book in place of "kingdom of God." Popularized by the theologian Ada María Isasi-Díaz, "kin-dom" is a more inclusive term that captures the reign of God better for many Christians than "kingdom" does.

nails in. In this moment of anagnorisis, progressive Christians have the opportunity to shift the tectonic plates of faith and politics in the United States. We have the opportunity to advance a just faith in the public square.

On November 9, 2016, I sat down at my dining room table with my laptop and started writing. My own lament turned into a passion for reckoning with how deeply broken Christian public engagement is in the United States. I wanted to do my part in helping shift those tectonic plates. For me, that meant more than sharing GIFs from the film *Saved!* or highlighting conservative Christian hypocrisy on Twitter. It meant sitting down the day after the election, bringing my background in writing and organizing to the work of reclaiming our faith.

The first draft of what became the book you're now holding (or reading on a tablet, #blessed) started as a memo on Christianity and public life. The memo was addressed to anyone trying their best to follow Jesus, yet about ready to give up on the word "Christian" because it has become so ugly. I circulated the memo to a few friends I'd worked with on faith-based public policy advocacy.

After a few months, the memo kept getting longer and longer, until it became this book. If you're still reading by this point, it's most likely that you're just as angry and depressed and just plain worn out as I am by the state of Christianity and public life in the United States today.

I've traveled around the country working at the intersection of progressive politics and religion for the past decade and met countless activists bogged down by un-Christlike conservativism prevailing in our public square. Headlines in the media about conservative Christians doubting climate change or supporting a wall on the southern border defy a third-grade Sunday school understanding of Christian social ethics. One of the saddest trends I've encountered is people of goodwill and conscience who work for social and economic justice in their communities and feel they can't identify as Christians any longer because they fear this self-identification will be taken the wrong way.

This book is for all of you.

This is my love letter to progressive Christians like you. And it's written out of a deep love and commitment to the cause of following Jesus in the transformative work his Sermon on the Mount calls us to live out. I'm so deeply inspired by your courage to stand for progressive values and follow Jesus in a culture that says Christians are gun-worshipping, gay-hating, fire-and-brimstone types. This book is for the Resistance who stepped into the streets to protest Trump because your faith demanded that you resist. It's for people whose devotion to God isn't about escaping hell, but about being called to co-create a just world.

> This is my love letter to progressive Christians like you. And it's written out of a deep love and commitment to the cause of following Jesus in the transformative work his Sermon on the Mount calls us to live out.

We've been counted out, worn out, and forced to answer for conservative Christians when we talk about being followers of Jesus. But we're not giving up. We have persisted in this culture despite the daunting circumstances. I don't believe we have to resign ourselves to the status quo for the rest of our lives.

My prayer for this book is that it strengthens you, your community, and our entire movement of progressive Christians for the work of healing the world.

In my travels I've met people of other faiths and of no faith who are distressed about the state of Christianity in the United States. This book is also for you, and I hope we can build partnerships for human dignity and the common good.

This book attempts to answer two big questions at the root of our current predicament: Where can we draw personal and collective inspiration for our work today as progressive Christians? And how do we reclaim our faith in the public square and shift the narrative of what it means to be a Christian in the United States?

Part One of this book is a reminder both of the bold tradition of progressive Christianity in the United States over the past hundred years and of the current state of those traditions in our country and world. It draws inspiration from Jesus's own *progressive* ministry and his radical message about pushing the boundaries of who was included in God's concern. It reminds us he preached a radical economic message of redistribution of wealth and called for us to love our enemies.

The two millennia of Christian history, like history in general, are full of progressive pushes forward and conservative reactions.

But in this book, I examine how we got ourselves into this current mess and look at the more recent story beginning about one hundred years ago—at the start of the twentieth century—when many, if not most, of the social reformers of this era were Christians. Theologians at that time formulated a new understanding of the "Social Gospel"—and were on the front lines of social and economic justice campaigns. Meanwhile, there was a huge evolution in theology as scholars questioned many aspects of Christian orthodoxy in light of scientific advances. As is the case with any evolutionary change, conservative Christians protested these changes.

The next great wave of progressive activism in the 1950s through the '70s also included many Christian activists and theologians in the civil rights movement, the anti-war movement, second-wave feminism, and the birth of liberation theologies. Yet again, conservative Christians fought back. This pushback was successful and gave rise to the religious right. From the 1980s until today, we've seen the religious right gain more and more cultural influence and religious progressives be nearly eradicated in the public square. The conservative Christian formulation of "secular liberalism" locked in a battle with religion became the popular cultural norm.

Conservative Christians cemented their lock on our public imagination in the 1990s and 2000s, just as I started to formulate my own understanding of Christian identity and belonging. Like me, a growing segment of the American population has been subjected to a Christian right agenda their entire lives. Looking at the longer history inspires us to rediscover our tradition of boldness and helps us determine how we got into the current predicament. I also find inspiration for my own development as a progressive Christian in my family's stories and in my work at the intersection of faith and politics.

Part Two of this book offers a plan for how progressive Christians can reclaim our tradition and demand our culture recognize the wide diversity of Christian beliefs today.

An exclusive new polling analysis provided by the Public Religion Research Institute sheds light on the comparative number of consistently progressive Christians and consistently conservative Christians in the United States. My own personal experience inside the highest reaches of conservative Christianity informs my analysis of how they win and how we can use that knowledge to shape our own strategies. One strategy that can't be minimized is the importance of being more vocal about how our faith informs our political views—even as there is also a healthy skepticism from both inside and outside of the world of progressive Christianity about being more vocal about our faith.

As Christians who believe in the power of the resurrection, in the power of good to overcome evil, we must find sources of hope in this work of reclaiming a just faith. My hope is found in the signs of progressive Christian revival that I see all over the country, such as the new Poor People's Campaign and the Nuns on the Bus activism. In the final chapter, Catholic activist and congresswoman Alexandria Ocasio-Cortez's "politics of love thy neighbor" gives us a strong role model to start reclaiming progressive Christianity.

My goal for this book is simple and straightforward: to make it a resource and conversation starter in progressive churches across the country, and for progressive Christians who have felt alienated from the church because of its conservative association. The theological and political commitments outlined in this book are not new, but they provide a new starting place by gathering these resources together in one place. I'm indebted to the many theologians and activists cited throughout the book. I'm also indebted to the integrated approach to analysis provided by the Wesleyan quadrilateral that I learned growing up in the Methodist Church, which has warmed my heart ever since: scripture, reason, tradition, and experience.

Ultimately, what I'm proposing is a new confidence and strategy for progressive Christians to live our faith publicly on our own terms. I hope this book is the beginning of a conversation with you, your community, your church, and the millions of progressive Christians around the country. Will we agree on every issue or tactic? Of course not. But we can all agree the status quo, where the average American hears the name of Jesus and immediately thinks about conservative causes, must be challenged. I'm hopeful that we can work together to change our public discourse about Christianity for the better.

★ PART ONE

OUR BOLD TRADITION

Then Jesus, filled with the power of the Spirit, returned to Galilee, and a report about him spread through all the surrounding country. He began to teach in their synagogues and was praised by everyone. When he came to Nazareth, where he had been brought up, he went to the synagogue on the sabbath day, as was his custom. He stood up to read, and the scroll of the prophet Isaiah was given to him. He unrolled the scroll and found the place where it was written:

"The Spirit of the Lord is upon me,
   because he has anointed me
   to bring good news to the poor.
He has sent me to proclaim release to the captives
   and recovery of sight to the blind,
   to let the oppressed go free,
to proclaim the year of the Lord's favor."

—Luke 4:14–19

When Jesus announces his ministry in Luke's Gospel, he roots himself in the tradition of the bold Hebrew prophets who spoke truth to power, sided with the poor against the rich, and envisioned a radical reorientation of society. Those on the bottom would be valued the most, and those on the top—the emperor, the rich, and their so-called "religious" co-conspirators— would face a reckoning for their active oppression.

Liberation is not some new cause Jesus invents, but one Jesus joins and draws people into to co-labor alongside him. Jesus the movement builder tells his followers in John's Gospel that they will do even greater works than he. The Acts of the Apostles is the story of the budding movement of Jesus's followers who shared all their possessions in common and brought into being the community Jesus preached about.

The bold tradition of people following Jesus to preach the good news that God is on the side of the vulnerable against the racist, sexist, and economic systems that limit human potential continues to this day. This is not the invention of some new form of Christianity, but joining in with the work of love that began before Jesus's ministry and extends throughout the history of people following him.

Even as progressives lay claim to a bold tradition that sides with the vulnerable and decries oppressive systems, in our American context today, conservative Christians portray themselves as the "traditional Christians" who resist any changes to their claimed tradition—whether it's scientific understanding of the world, LGBTQ rights, or the country's growing non-white population. Progress and change are pitted against tradition by many conservative Christians. That's not surprising. Progressives have not always been met with acceptance or welcome from the official church structures. But then again, official religious institutions didn't get too high a grade from Jesus.

It's important to contest what it means to be "traditional." What conservative Christians wield as a bludgeoning tool can obstruct progress. We need to recall how "tradition" was weaponized to resist ordaining women and to sanction slavery. But more important is finding the tradition of progressive Christianity inspiring to our work in the world today. Every time I encounter an example of Christians who put their faith into action for the common good, it inspires me to do the same. I hope that the long tradition of faith informing the common good is inspiration for you, too.

We need to wrestle with the past, not view it as some trophy on a mantel. Where our ancestors in the bold tradition of progressive Christianity erred, let us learn from our mistakes and move forward. One of the hallmarks of progressive Christianity is our openness to change. We don't need to "go back" or "Make Christianity Great Again," but we can be inspired by the past.

There are competing traditions in Christian history, and this is not an attempt to say who the "real Christians" were at any point in history or in the present. There were self-identified followers of Jesus who launched the Crusades and turned the Jesus movement into a chaplaincy for empire. There continue to be self-identified followers of Jesus who think the earth was *literally* created in six twenty-four-hour days, want to control women's reproductive freedom, cover up and excuse the horrors of capitalism, and make justifications for America's endless wars in the Middle East. That's their "tradition."

What's strange is that conservative Christians claim to have a monopoly on "tradition." This book has been written in part to correct the record, to denounce the lies, and to recall the bold tradition of progressive Christianity, because while we are continuing to courageously advance our faith tradition, we can draw on a long line of people who have sought that same thing.

Families, like religions, pass down traditions. My family raised me in the bold tradition of progressive Christianity. My grandmother, Frances Bell Graves, who died while I was writing this book and to whom it is dedicated, was more devoted to her Christian faith than any person I've ever encountered. I cherish the memory of her teaching me to memorize the Lord's Prayer as a child and encouraging me in my faith as a youth. Her commitment to social justice sprang out of her daily prayer life and work as a missionary in Mexico. She volunteered at Casa Juan Diego, the Catholic Worker House in my hometown of Houston, and she marched alongside my union organizer parents and me in anti-war and labor union protests.

My path to writing this book is rooted in my upbringing, just as all of our ongoing struggles for social and economic justice are rooted in the activism that came before us. This is not to say my childhood religious experiences were all perfect or that any movement that came before us got everything right. But I am grateful to have my own personal experience of traditional Christianity actually looking something like the words Jesus quotes from Isaiah in the Luke 4 passage above.

Jesus drew on the tradition of the bold Hebrew prophets who came before him. But there was certainly a conservative religious element of his own time as well. The passage that began this section goes on to record Jesus saying in verse 24: "Truly I tell you, no prophet is accepted in the prophet's hometown." Then the Gospel of Luke records in verse 29–30 that those listening "got up, drove him out of the town, and led him to the brow of the hill on which their town was built, so that they might hurl him off the cliff. But he passed through the midst of them and went on his way."

From the very beginning of Jesus's ministry, through more than two thousand years of Christian history, to right now as you're reading this book, there have been competing understandings of how religious values should inform our personal and social lives. People have put their faith into action whether for the common good or to maintain the status quo by hurling threats off a cliff. Conservative Christians have their tradition. We have our own.

There will be moments of tension like the one recounted here in Luke's Gospel. Let's follow Jesus's example here and calmly go on our way. Let's go on our way to bring good news to the poor by ending poverty. Let's go on our way to proclaim release to the captives and abolish private prisons. Let's go on our way to free the oppressed and proclaim the year of the Lord's favor. Let's go on our way to proclaim that Black Lives Matter and not be deterred by conservative Christians responding "All

Lives Matter" to deflect the serious harms of racism. Let's go on our way to demand health care for all when critics say "it costs too much" until the moment a pandemic hits. Let's go on our way and draw inspiration from those who have gone before us.

CHAPTER 1

SHALL THE FUNDAMENTALISTS KEEP WINNING?

This book focuses on the type of progressive Christian political engagement championed by Rev. Dr. Martin Luther King Jr. and many others in the public square and outside the walls of the church. Entering the story of progressive Christianity in the United States in the midst of a theological battle might seem like an odd choice. But our views on theological battles have a profound effect on our social witness in the public square. Those of us interested in reforming society often have a keen interest in reforming the church to live up to the same values we champion outside its walls. Jesus calls us to champion the same values of inclusion, reason, and justice in our own religious institutions and in society as a whole.

Of course, theology and politics are not the same thing. The history of progressive Catholics in the United States and Vatican II is a good example of this dynamic. Vatican II opened up the church to theological reforms like saying the Mass in languages other than Latin. The theological modernization that happened with Vatican II is distinct from the long history of the Catholic Left, such as the Catholic Worker Movement and liberation theology, but it presented a symbiotic relationship between the push to reform the Catholic Church and the push for social justice in society. On the other side of the equation, the conservative Catholic movement's theology and politics of exclusion are mutually reinforcing. So too is this the case for American Protestants.

The modernist-fundamentalist tension of the early twentieth century is still raging today. Don't take it from me, but from my Louisville, Kentucky, neighbor Albert (Al) Mohler. I have more in common with Al, president of the Southern Baptist Theological Seminary, than you might expect. We're not just white, male Christians of the Baptist variety in Louisville who are interested in the intersection of faith and public life. No, we have something much more important in common. We both believe that the fundamentalist-modernist controversy is still raging today. We may be on opposite sides of the divide, but we both identify it as the defining divide of American Protestantism, even though some of the language articulating that controversy has changed since the 1920s.

"We're back in the same pattern," Mohler said during an interview with historian Frances FitzGerald. "Many historians speak of the conservative movement in the [Southern Baptist Convention] and describe it as fundamentalist. And by the way in terms of spirit, I think there's legitimacy to that; I say that as a conservative Southern Baptist," Mohler said while noting there are some differences between modern evangelicals and their fundamentalist predecessors.[1]

The people known as "evangelicals" today are the descendants of fundamentalists and carry on the tradition of conservative Christianity. On the other side, there are those of us who don't feel tied to defending the status quo, largely self-identifying as "progressive Christians" today. And understanding the history of the fundamentalist-modernist divide is essential to understanding American Protestantism today.

Modernists accepted the truth of evolution (shocking!) and used the historical-critical method of Biblical studies to reevaluate Christian teaching in light of new evidence. These ideas were rejected by the fundamentalists, who refused to see reason as itself a gift from our Creator. The fundamentalist-modernist controversy, boiled down to its essential elements, was a rebellion against the natural and social sciences by a fearful and reactionary force in the Protestant churches. It's one reason the descendants of fundamentalists today—evangelicals—so easily embraced a president who claimed climate change is a "Chinese hoax." This shouldn't have come as a surprise.

Nineteenth-century liberal theologians—first in Germany with the father of theological liberalism, German theologian Friedrich Schleiermacher, and then on both sides of the Atlantic—began integrating the natural and social sciences into their theological work and biblical scholarship. This process slowly advanced throughout the second half of the nineteenth century and reached a head in different US Protestant denominations throughout the twentieth century. Al Mohler would himself help lead a purge of liberals and moderates from the Southern Baptist Convention that took place from the late 1970s to the early 1990s.

The modernist-fundamentalist controversy blew up in the 1920s in the Presbyterian Church in the United States of America (PCUSA), which, as it so happens, is now based in Louisville. (Wherever you go in my city, this controversy lingers!) Though the fight took place primarily in that denomination, similar debates played out in all of American Protestantism. If Twitter had existed at the time, there would have been quite a few GIFs of houses on fire. The authority of Scripture, the resurrection, the atonement, the virgin birth, and many other Christian hot topics were up all for debate in churches and the public square.

> Today "fundamentalism" has come into common usage to mean a strict resistance to change in any religious context, but . . . it derives from a series of pamphlets called "The Fundamentals."

Princeton Theological Seminary professor Gresham Machen was one of the most prominent fundamentalists concerned by the theological liberalism growing in his Presbyterian denomination. He ultimately left the denomination and seminary to found the Orthodox Presbyterian Church and the Westminster Theological Seminary.

Today "fundamentalism" has come into common usage to mean a strict resistance to change in any religious context, but at that time the word was new. It derives from a series of pamphlets called "The Fundamentals," financed by a wealthy Presbyterian named Lyman Stewart.

The pamphlets set forth a series of nonnegotiable points that Christians were to agree on or face charges of heresy. The two most important arguments for fundamentalists were and continue to be the inerrancy of the Bible, meaning everything in the Bible is true, and reading the Bible literally. Fundamentalists invented this new menu of irrefutable beliefs as a response to the higher criticism of the Bible by liberal theologians. Any new information that might call previous views into question was not just rejected, but new lines of exclusion were developed to protect the old beliefs that were being challenged.

This push for inerrancy and a literal reading of the Bible was a fear-based reaction to a perception that theological liberalism had opened a whole can of worms in its openness to the natural and social sciences. The push for a literal reading is indefensible to anyone who opens the Bible and sees different points of view, storytelling approaches, and literary traditions. Two contradictory creation stories open Genesis: one describes God creating the world in six days; the other describes God creating the garden of Eden. You can deny science and affirm both stories, but it's prima facie impossible to say both are *literally* true.

Fundamentalists drew a hard line around a few specific beliefs beyond their general affirmation of inerrancy and literal reading of the Bible: Jesus literally performed miracles, Mary was literally a virgin when she conceived Jesus, a bodily resurrection will literally take place when all the dead Christians inherit the earth upon the physical return of Christ, and Jesus was literally a substitutionary atonement on the cross—paying a blood ransom to satisfy God's vengeance for the sins of humanity.

These issues—like same-sex marriage and criminalizing abortion today—were selected by fundamentalists not out of a long history of Christian tradition, but as a reaction to new thinking and societal change. Fundamentalism then and now—like conservative politics—revolves around a strict sense of social control and maintaining "order," claiming that as the highest form of ethics. The modernists of the 1920s and 1930s stood up and fought this "traditional" mindset.

The Contentious Formation of the Riverside Church

Harry Emerson Fosdick graduated from New York City's Union Theological Seminary in 1904 and went through a theological transformation while studying there. "I no longer believed the old stuff I had been taught. Moreover, I no longer merely doubted it. I rose in indignant revolt against it," he wrote in his autobiography.[2] Ordained as a Baptist minister, he was installed as preaching minister at New York's First Presbyterian Church. There he preached one of the most famous sermons in American history—and lost his job because of it. As the fundamentalist-modernist controversy built in its intensity, Fosdick delivered a sermon titled "Shall the Fundamentalists Win?"

The Fundamentalists see, and they see truly, that in this last generation there have been strange new movements in Christian thought. A great mass of new knowledge has come into man's possession—new knowledge about the physical universe, its origin, its forces, its laws; new knowledge about human history and in particular about the ways in which the ancient peoples used to think in matters of religion and the methods by which they phrased and explained their spiritual experiences; and new knowledge, also, about other religions and the strangely similar ways in which men's faiths and religious practices have developed everywhere.[3]

For Christians today, it's hard to imagine a time before evangelicals were pitted against secular liberals. But there was a very fruitful and evolving sense of Christianity as informed by new advances in science and philosophy. People's understanding of Christianity was changing, but it didn't make them any less Christian.

Fosdick's sermon wasn't even a full-throated defense of liberalism but, rather, a defense of the freedom to believe differently and not limit the freedom of conscience of Christians. For fundamentalists who would not tolerate the widening range of different thinking, however, it came off as a defense of liberalism. Fundamentalism saw it as a refusal to submit to the authority of the fundamentals. They rallied their supporters to defend the borders of acceptable thought and expelled anyone who disagreed.

"The trouble was, of course, that in stating the liberal and fundamentalist positions, I had stood in a Presbyterian pulpit and said frankly what the modernist position on some points was—the virgin birth no longer accepted as historic fact, the literal inerrancy of the Scriptures incredible, the second coming of Christ from the skies an outmoded phrasing of hope," Fosdick later wrote.[4]

Not long after he preached the sermon, the fundamentalists conspired to force him out of the pulpit at the First Presbyterian Church of New York. Fosdick was then called as pastor at Park Avenue Baptist Church in 1925, which changed its name to the Riverside Church when a new building was funded by member John D. Rockefeller Jr. and completed in 1930. It quickly became considered the citadel of progressive Christianity. Several legacies came through Fosdick's approach to battling the fundamentalists, getting kicked out of the Presbyterian Church, and developing his own non-creedal interdenominational church next door to Union Seminary, where he also taught as a professor.

Fosdick's first legacy was that he modeled a boldness that continued in Riverside Church and the larger progressive Christian movement. "Well, they are not going to do it; certainly not in this vicinity," was Fosdick's defiant answer to the fundamentalists.[5] "I do not even know in this congregation whether anybody has been tempted to be a Fundamentalist. Never in this church have I caught one accent of intolerance. God keep us always so and ever increasing areas of the Christian fellowship;

intellectually hospitable, open-minded, liberty-loving, fair, tolerant, not with the tolerance of indifference, as though we did not care about the faith, but because always our major emphasis is upon the weightier matters of the law."[6]

Another legacy Fosdick gave the progressive faith tradition was a model for self-reflection and a criticism of his own tribe.

When will the world learn that intolerance solves no problems? This is not a lesson which the Fundamentalists alone need to learn; the liberals also need to learn it. Speaking, as I do, from the viewpoint of liberal opinions, let me say that if some young, fresh mind here this morning is holding new ideas, has fought his way through, it may be by intellectual and spiritual struggle, to novel positions, and is tempted to be intolerant about old opinions, offensively to condescend to those who hold them and to be harsh in judgment on them, he may well remember that people who held those old opinions have given the world some of the noblest character and the most rememberable service that it ever has been blessed with, and that we of the younger generation will prove our case best, not by controversial intolerance, but by producing, with our new opinions, something of the depth and strength, nobility and beauty of character that in other times were associated with other thoughts. It was a wise liberal, the most adventurous man of his day—Paul the Apostle— who said, "Knowledge puffeth up, but love buildeth up."[7]

Fosdick's appeal to the Apostle Paul as a liberal is perhaps surprising to readers today. Progressive Christians today have largely given up on Paul because, despite some radical love passages in the Epistles, there are also "clobber" verses cited by fundamentalists to promote hatred of women and the LGBTQ community. However, as we'll see in chapter 3, another progressive, Rev. Dr. Martin Luther King Jr., calls Paul an extremist—a compliment coming from King.

Coming to the words of Fosdick as a gay Christian, I have appreciated his modeling of how to not be "intolerant about old opinions" since many people, like himself, were on a continuum and changing their minds. Where the temptation is to be intolerant in return, Fosdick instead supports words spoken from conscience, with respect to others who may disagree.

The third legacy Fosdick left progressives was that he was able to connect the theological and political dimensions of progressive Christianity. "The present world situation smells to heaven! And now, in the presence of colossal problems, which must be solved in Christ's name and for Christ's sake, the Fundamentalists propose to drive out from the Christian churches all the consecrated souls who do not agree with their theory of inspiration. What immeasurable folly!"[8] Today we see a version of that dilemma, with fundamentalists focused on literal biblical readings and ideological purity, while progressive Christians are focused on the political and social problems of the world.

Finally, Fosdick had the insight to leverage the new media approaches of his time. Had he been living today, he surely would have been on the vanguard of social media approaches. He distributed his sermon in pamphlet form to ministers across the nation. Not only did Fosdick focus on print; he was an early adopter of radio to broadcast his sermons from Riverside across the country.

During the 1920s and 1930s, the modernists and moderates largely won the debate in the Protestant denominations. The Southern Baptist Convention in the 1980s was the sole victory of the fundamentalists—and the fundamentalists retreated to form breakaway denominations. In fact, the modernist/liberal denominations became so powerful that they were called "mainline Protestant" as distinct from the fundamentalists who were out on the fringes. But the battles never went away.

The same battles between liberalism and fundamentalism are playing out today. Liberal Christianity has continued to evolve over time as new information becomes available, science advances, and we who are followers of Christ grow through our lived experience.

Sometimes, the battles look eerily similar to those of the 1920s. In 2019, controversy again broke out about the affirmation of a literal resurrection and virgin birth, and the absence of such affirmation signaling heresy. Union Theological Seminary's current and first female president, Rev. Dr. Serene Jones, came under intense scrutiny on Easter that year for refusing to affirm either.

"I find the virgin birth a bizarre claim," Jones told *New York Times* columnist Nicholas Kristof. "It has nothing to do with Jesus' message. The virgin birth only becomes important if you have a theology in which sexuality is considered sinful. It also promotes this notion that the pure, untouched female body is the best body, and that idea has led to centuries of oppressing women."[9]

When Kristof followed up by asking Jones, "For someone like myself who is drawn to Jesus' teaching but doesn't believe in the virgin birth or the physical resurrection, what am I? Am I a Christian?" Jones responded, "Well, you sound an awful lot like me, and I'm a Christian minister."[10]

The column led to mass hysteria that sounded strangely like the debates from the 1920s. The only difference was that people were shocked to learn a Christian minister wouldn't affirm the physical resurrection. There seemed to be surprise at the very existence of theological liberals. During the fundamentalist-modernist controversy, Jones's statement would have surely been considered heretical by the fundamentalists. A woman serving as president of a seminary would have been heretical, too. But the existence of theological liberals would not have been a surprise to anyone. They were openly battling the fundamentalists!

Many of the debates between modernism and fundamentalism have changed over time as each has shifted and evolved. Fundamentalism has been rebranded as evangelicalism and modernism has been influenced by postmodern, post-colonial, and other forms of theology like liberation theology. But the two streams of evolving/progressive faith and conservative/reactionary faith have made consistent appeals and are heirs to the same traditions.

Today two of the biggest fights over evolving theology concern women's reproductive health care and the holiness of LGBTQ people. The theological debates over both concern different "clobber passages" of the Bible cited by fundamentalists. For LGBTQ rights, the focus is on six passages: Genesis 19, Leviticus 18:22, Leviticus 20:13, 1 Corinthians 6:9–10, 1 Timothy 1:10, and Romans 1:26–27. Concerning women's reproductive health care and criminalizing abortion, anti-abortion activists cite Psalm 139 and Jeremiah 1:5. Fundamentalists weaponize these few verses even though their positions on both LGBTQ rights and abortion have existed for a tiny fraction of Christian history. This evolution has taken a long time, even in the progressive tradition. The lack of openness to the role of LGBTQ people in the church has been especially painful over the past few decades as every denomination, just as they faced the modernist-fundamentalist controversy, has had to decide if they would be open to changing their minds on an issue of vast importance to people on both sides of the debate.

"What present-day critics of liberalism often fail to see is its absolute necessity to multitudes of us who would not have been Christians at all unless we could thus have escaped the bondage of the then reigning orthodoxy," Fosdick wrote in his autobiography.[11] Without the push by progressive Christians to reform our faith tradition, many of us wouldn't be Christian. But thankfully, many, like Fosdick, have stayed and fought the fundamentalists and given us a robust tradition to follow.

I entered Union Theological Seminary, where Fosdick attended and taught, on a scholarship in the field of Christian social ethics named for William Sloane Coffin, one of Fosdick's successors as senior minister of the Riverside Church. I had to change my own denominational affiliation because the United Methodist Church didn't embrace the role of LGBTQ people in the church. I wanted to be in a church where I could serve openly and marry in my church. In an unlikely turn I became a Baptist, moving to a tradition where each individual church decides its position.

There is no doubt that fundamentalists have harmed a lot of people—especially women, queer people, and people of color. The #exvangelical movement has generated attention in the past couple of years by highlighting people leaving evangelicalism in the age of Trump. Every time we think of the damage done by fundamentalists' harmful positions, we might also lift up Christians who have stayed and reformed our religious tradition for the better.

We've stayed because we're committed to following Jesus and we're not willing to give up the fight and let the fundamentalists win. Whenever Jesus says something in the Gospels responding to a critic, we're reminded of our own critics in real life. One of Jesus's most famous critics appears in the Gospel of Matthew. Jesus answered him, saying, "Do not think that I have come to abolish the law or the prophets; I have come not to abolish but to fulfill" (5:17). The fear-based reaction by the religious leaders of his time considered Jesus a threat to the status quo. His prophetic ministry was dismissed under the guise of tradition. Maybe that sounds similar to the fundamentalists' accusations about progressive Christians today.

Jesus of Nazareth lived, died, and lived again as an itinerant Jewish preacher. He never founded his own religion, nor did he destroy what came before him. Only later did Christianity and Judaism diverge. Similarly, for progressive Christians in the 1920s, the goal was not to create a new tradition or religious expression, but to live that bold expression in new ways and in their own context. The same is true of progressive Christians today. Those who consider themselves progressive Christians now are confidently living faith in an ongoing expression of a long and bold tradition. Sometimes the people of that Christian expression have been labeled heretics, which carries a kinship to Jesus acting out of love, concern, and justice and being labeled a heretic by the religious leaders of his own day.

> For progressive Christians in the 1920s, the goal was not to create a new tradition or religious expression, but to live that bold expression in new ways and in their own context.

Fosdick was labeled a heretic for embracing the liberal Christians' right to exist in the church, even if he did not side with every liberal view. By understanding our history, we can reclaim a tradition of boldness and lean into labels of heresy today, as Fosdick did in his time. Our current "heresies" are believing science, the dignity of women and the LGBQ community, taking the Bible seriously but not literally, advocating for social justice, and joining God in the cause of liberation for the poor and people of color. If getting labeled a heretic is what following Jesus costs us, then let people call us heretics.

In the tradition of Fosdick and the progressive movement he represented, the Riverside Church continued to evolve over time, embracing the progressive movement at every turn. But among Fosdick's other gifts to the church is the well-known hymn "God of Grace and God of Glory"—the memorable words of which are still sung by churches:

> God of grace and God of glory,
> on your people pour your power;
> crown your ancient church's story,
> bring its bud to glorious flower.
> Grant us wisdom, grant us courage,
> for the facing of this hour,
> for the facing of this hour.[12]

When Rev. Dr. Martin Luther King Jr. inscribed a copy of *Stride toward Freedom*, his account of the 1955–56 Montgomery Bus Boycott, for Fosdick, he wrote these words: "If I were called upon to select the foremost prophets of our generation, I would choose you to head the list."[13] "For the facing of this hour" in 2020 and beyond, my hope for Christian progressives is that we may draw inspiration from "the ancient church's story" and continue to "bring its bud to glorious flower." And my prayer continues to be for the church: God, grant us wisdom and courage.

CHAPTER 2

THE NEW DEAL, GREEN NEW DEAL, AND CHRISTIAN NEW DEAL

Social justice and Christian ethics are two sides of the same coin, both as a matter of historical context and in my own faith story. My first memory of church wasn't at my home church, which was a mostly white, liberal congregation of the United Methodist Church in Houston. I was six years old when I established my earliest memory at a church. I was at a much larger, predominantly black church in another neighborhood accompanying my father, who was then working on the campaign to raise the minimum wage in Houston to $6.50. This was 1996–1997 and long before the $15 minimum wage standard we fight for today. We stood outside the church passing out leaflets for the campaign.

Black churches were some of the most active supporters of the minimum wage campaign because black churches and the broader black community have been some of the most influential sites of economic and racial justice organizing in America. As the son of two community and labor union organizers, I spent a large part of my childhood as an organizer-in-training, helping out around the union office and accompanying my parents to sign up members at their workplaces.

Growing up, the Bible stories I read in church about Jesus turning tables for economic justice mirrored what I saw my parents doing by helping workers gain a voice in their workplaces. Looking back, I see a child simultaneously taught two approaches to accomplishing the same ultimate goal of a just society.

God's investment in social justice is revealed in even the most cursory reading of the Bible. The Hebrew Bible begins with the radical idea that creation is good and that all people are made in the image of God. God delivers the Israelites out of captivity. The prophets call out injustice and proclaim a radical hope for the future when justice and peace will abound. The Jewish tradition of *tzedakah*—justice or righteousness in Hebrew—continues to inspire the bold tradition of progressive Jewish advocacy that we see today with groups like Bend the Arc, Jewish Voice for Peace, and the Jewish Social Justice Roundtable.

Christians draw upon the long tradition of justice in the Hebrew Bible as well as in the New Testament, which itself offers no shortage of social justice passages. The apostle Paul declares a radical equality—"there is no longer slave or free, there is no longer male and female" (Gal 3:28)—in the early Jesus movement. And he furthers the focus of the early church sharing all possessions in common in Acts. But for progressive Christians, one passage stands out in particular and tends to be the most referenced: Matthew 25:31–46. The passage is the starkest example in the Gospels of how God judges. If we are commanded by Jesus to love God and neighbor, then Matthew 25 fleshes out the rubric of how well we carry out that commandment, which will be judged.

In contrast to the conservative Christian focus on "saving souls" from eternal conscious torment in hell, progressives return to Matthew 25, where Jesus builds on the long history of Jewish theology holding salvation as a collective endeavor for the nation rather than an individualistic pursuit.

Jesus tells his disciples that at the end of history, when the Son of Man reigns, "all the nations will be gathered before him, and he will separate people one from another as a shepherd separates the sheep from the goats, and he will put the sheep at his right hand and the goats at the left" (Matt 25:32–33). Jesus gives his disciples a simple rubric for how the nations will be judged in terms of how they treated their neighbor, and that how they treated the most vulnerable directly reflected how they treated him. He uses first-person language to drive home the point:

- ■ "I was hungry and you gave me food,
- ■ "I was thirsty and you gave me something to drink,
- ■ "I was a stranger and you welcomed me,
- ■ "I was naked and you gave me clothing,
- ■ "I was sick and you took care of me,
- ■ "I was in prison and you visited me." (Matt 25:35–36)

The sheep, which we might think of as stand-ins for Jesus's followers, don't understand. They don't remember Jesus ever needing to be visited in prison or hungry and needing food. When they ask Jesus about this, he responds in verse 40, "Truly I tell you, just as you did it to one of the least of these who are members of my family, you did it to me." The goats—the people who did not welcome the stranger or visit the sick—are sent away for eternal punishment.

Judging a society based on how the most vulnerable are treated isn't just the foundation of the progressive Christian social witness, but the entire idea of what we call the "progressive movement" in the United States. It's why we judge the economy not based on how the top one percent are faring, but rather on how much better we as a society have made life for the poor and working class. It's why we measure the cost of war in terms of lives lost on both sides and why we refuse to allow torture or other means of violence that degrades the dignity of humanity.

> Judging a society based on how the most vulnerable are treated isn't just the foundation of the progressive Christian social witness, but the entire idea of what we call the "progressive movement" in the United States.

It's why we work for racial justice and support reparations so we can finally have reckoning as a nation about the evil of slavery. It's why we fight for health care as a human right and fight to reform our criminal justice system.

For many Christians, this Matthew 25 passage encapsulates what our aims as a society should be, and it has informed and rooted those active in social and economic justice movements.

Today, we mostly think of social justice as a secular movement sometimes associated with progressive causes that are fighting the "Christian right" and other conservative groups. But many of the original "social justice warriors" in the United States were themselves deeply rooted in their Christian faith and drew inspiration from the Bible and such passages as Matthew 25.

Even the highly secularized term "social justice" was originally coined by a Jesuit priest. There's a rich history of social justice within the Catholic Church, including both official church documents like Pope Leo XIII's *Rerum Novarum* in 1891 and grassroots Catholic activism that includes when Dorothy Day started the Catholic Worker Movement in 1932.

For Protestants, Walter Rauschenbusch was the foremost theologian of the Social Gospel movement, which fought to advance both economic and social justice, focusing on issues of poverty, alcoholism, racism, the environment, child labor, labor unions, and public education. A Baptist minister in Hell's Kitchen in New York City, Rauschenbusch saw firsthand the terrible living conditions of the urban poor. He identified following Jesus with transforming society to make it more equitable and just. "[The kingdom of God] is not a matter of getting individuals to heaven, but of transforming the life on earth into the harmony of heaven," Rauschenbusch wrote in his highly influential 1907 book *Christianity and Social Crisis*.[14] This tagline of the progressive Christian movement runs through every issue we advocate for, whether it's environmental protection, anti-racism work, public health advocacy, or anything else. "The better we know Jesus, the more social do his thoughts and aims become," Rauschenbusch wrote. "Whoever uncouples the religious and social life has not understood Jesus. Whoever sets any bounds for the reconstructive power of the religious life over the social relations and institutions of men, to that extent denies the faith of the Master."[15]

Rauschenbusch and his fellow Social Gospelers paved the way for the social justice movement as we understand it today. Their Protestant appeals for justice, along with Catholic appeals and Jewish appeals together combined to inspire the progressive movement today. They've been joined along the way by progressive people of faith in other religious traditions.

One of the most famous social and economic justice warriors in American history has been Franklin Delano Roosevelt. According to a survey of presidential politics experts, FDR is the greatest president of the twentieth century and trails only Abraham Lincoln and George Washington among all US presidents.[16] He is the overwhelming favorite of experts to be the next carved into Mt. Rushmore.

When we talk about "progressive" presidents, FDR first comes to mind. His administration advanced bold economic reforms as part of the New Deal during the Great Depression, reforms only rivaled by Lyndon Johnson's Great Society programs for the government intervention that progressives believe is necessary to ensure a basic quality of life for all Americans. Lest there be too much idealization of an imperfect man and administration, it's important to name the ways in which FDR did not live up to progressive values: interning Japanese Americans during World War II and making compromises with racist members of Congress to pass the New Deal.

While my Democratic family idolized FDR as I was growing up, I never saw him as a religious figure until I read a spiritual biography about him, which explored FDR's Christian convictions. As someone who asks Democrats to take religion more seriously, I regularly reference the faith of Barack Obama, John Lewis, Nancy Pelosi, Hillary Clinton, Ilhan Omar, and Elizabeth Warren, to name a few, but FDR is a hero to many Democrats today, and the conviction of his faith provided groundwork for those who followed after him. Even with all the work I've done to advance the causes of progressive people of faith, I still find myself constantly surprised by the religious narratives around progressive figures but often hidden from view.

"Franklin Roosevelt was launched from the cradle on a religious trajectory," according to historians John F. Woolverton and James D. Bratt, who wrote *A Christian and a Democrat: A Religious Biography of Franklin D. Roosevelt.*[17] "As a child and a youth, he was brought up in the church. He knew and ever treasured its hymns, liturgy, Scripture, and prayers. Through his father, his Swiss governess, and later his wife, Eleanor, the Social Gospel and its causes in the Progressive Era became his."

As president, FDR "rallied a solid majority of American citizens to a vision of justice and democracy that came right out of

Scripture—and his heritage of liberal Protestantism."[18] Once, he was pointedly asked about the source of his political philosophy at a press conference. "Momentarily dumbfounded, he replied that he was a Christian and a Democrat."[19]

The Social Gospel movement also inspired several prominent members of his administration. Harry Hopkins was perhaps the most influential person aside from FDR in developing the New Deal. He was the head of the Federal Emergency Relief Administration, the Civil Works Administration, and the Works Progress Administration, each of the governmental bodies responsible for building out the New Deal.

"Hopkins became not only his relief administrator but his general assistant as no one had been able to be," FDR's Labor Secretary Frances Perkins wrote in her book *The Roosevelt I Knew*.[20] "Roosevelt was greatly enriched by Hopkins's knowledge, ability, and humane attitude towards all facets of life." June Hopkins later wrote about her grandfather Harry Hopkins that he embraced the Social Gospel movement while studying at Grinnell College. "The intertwining of theology and ethics with politics and sociology at Grinnell College, so distinct in progressive reform, suggests a religious framework for Hopkins' social conscience."[21]

For FDR, that framework was similarly informed: "FDR's view of God's future for humankind was expressed in terms of social progress," Woolverton and Bratt write. "In accord with what appeared to him to be God's testament in Jesus Christ, with the confidence in the potential in all humanity, and with the conviction that progress demanded boldness on the new administration's part, Roosevelt in his inaugural address of 1933 promised 'direct, vigorous action.' The Social Gospel ideas of Perkins, Harry Hopkins, Henry Wallace, Eleanor Roosevelt, and their associates were about to be tested."[22]

They were certainly tested, but not only did those ideas succeed in getting the country out of the Great Depression; they also proved to be the lasting foundation for Democrats well into the twenty-first century.

The most direct link between the New Deal and today's progressive leaders is the call for a Green New Deal. The proposal, which was formally introduced in the United States House of Representatives by Congresswoman Alexandria Ocasio-Cortez and in the United States Senate by Senator Edward Markey on February 7, 2019, addresses the twin concerns of climate change and income inequality. The Green New Deal as initially proposed would guarantee a job with a "family-sustaining wage" to all people of the United States and meet 100% of the power demand in the United States through clean, renewable, and zero-emission energy sources, among many other economic and environmental goals.

The Social Gospel cause that undergirded the original New Deal during FDR's time continues to inspire Christian supporters of the Green New Deal today. The environmental movement in the United States has counted many Christians among its members, and today some of the most prominent champions of taking action to combat climate change cite their faith as inspiration—including Representative Alexandria Ocasio-Cortez. She has become one of the most influential leaders in the country not just on the environment, but also on the entire progressive movement. She has occasionally quoted Bible verses on Twitter and wrote an op-ed for the Catholic magazine *America*.[23] In one exchange that made national news, Ocasio-Cortez got in a Christian dustup with then–White House Press Secretary Sarah Huckabee Sanders. "I don't think we're going to listen to her on much of anything, particularly not on matters we're gonna leave in the hands of a much, much higher authority," Sanders said on the FOX News *Hannity* show.[24] Ocasio-Cortez responded by appealing to the Bible on Twitter: "Genesis 1: God looked on the world & called it good not once, not twice, but seven times. Genesis 2: God commands all people to 'serve and protect' creation. Leviticus: God mandates that not only the people, but the land that sustains them, shall be respected."[25] The interaction drew a sharp distinction about how progressive Christians like Ocasio-Cortez and conservative Christians like Sanders view our responsibility for social justice.

Other environmental activists cite their Christian faith as well, such as Bill McKibben, Al Gore, and Dr. Katherine Hayhoe. "I do my best to read the signs of the times, and in our day and age it often means listening hard to what scientists have to tell us," McKibben told Religion News Service.[26] Gore, who briefly attended Vanderbilt Divinity School but did not graduate, has said that "I believe that the purpose of life is to glorify God—and if we heap contempt and destruction on God's creation, that is grotesquely inconsistent with the way we are supposed to be living our lives.[27] Dr. Katherine Hayhoe is a prominent climate science and self-proclaimed evangelical Christian. "I chose what to study precisely because of my faith, because climate change disproportionately affects the poor and vulnerable, those already most at risk today," she wrote in a *New York Times* op-ed. "To me, caring about and acting on climate was a way to live out my calling to love others as we've been loved ourselves by God."[28]

Environmental action and income inequality are two of the most vital concerns for progressive people of faith today, and just as we draw inspiration from the New Deal, we should see how the Social Gospel inspired the New Deal and can help get us to the Green New Deal. The Social Gospel lays the same call on us as Christians as it did a hundred years ago: bring heaven to earth by co-creating with God a more just and equitable society. It's the work of leaders like Rep. Alexandria Ocasio-Cortez and Eleanor Roosevelt, but it's also the work of all of us who follow Jesus.

CHAPTER 3

THE "REVEREND" IN
REV. DR. KING

Black voters, and black women voters in particular, are the most likely voters in the American electorate to vote Democratic. That's not surprising and is often commented on in our public discourse. Yet when it comes to faith and politics, the American electorate is often broken down by pollsters via a racialized lens into the following subcategories of "Christian": white evangelical Protestant, white mainline Protestant, Catholic, black Protestant, and other Christians. There was endless, mind-numbing commentary about the 81% of white evangelicals who voted for Donald Trump in 2016, according to exit polls. But of the categories I mentioned, white evangelicals are considered the most loyal religious bloc to any party. Yet, according to a pre-election survey, 90% of black Protestants planned to vote for Hillary Clinton and just 3% for Donald Trump.[29]

American public discourse has a racist tendency to emphasize the religious motivations of white Christians and deemphasize the religious motivations of black Christians. Any discussion of American politics that highlights the "black vote" and the "white evangelical vote" as two constituencies is picking and choosing whose faith matters and is warping our public imagination of Christianity in favor of conservative Christians.

In 2014 a special issue of *Smithsonian Magazine* listed the one hundred most significant people in United States history. In that list was Rev. Dr. Martin Luther King Jr. And along with George Washington, he was the only American leader to have his birthday recognized as a federal holiday. But, curiously, *Smithsonian* categorized King under the heading of "Rebels & Resisters" alongside Robert E. Lee, Thomas Paine, Susan B. Anthony, and Elizabeth Cady Stanton.[30] While listing confederates in the same category as civil rights activists can make a progressive wince, what is also striking about King in this category is that he was the only clergyperson.

In a separate category listing "Religious Figures," *Smithsonian* did not list King, but featured eleven white people, among them Mormon leader Joseph Smith, Scientology founder L. Ron Hubbard, and evangelist Billy Graham. Billy Graham was frequently called "America's pastor," which didn't come with a rebel or resister label, nor did those eleven figures significantly disrupt power systems in the United States.

The Rev. Dr. King is most often viewed today as an activist rather than a religious figure, even though his lifelong profession was that of church pastor. Erasing King's religiosity isn't some kind of anomaly but part of this racist tradition of whom we label "religious" today. This tradition extends back before King to the time period discussed in the previous chapter.

At the same time as the Rauschenbusch-inspired Social Gospel movement, a parallel but distinct stream in black churches in the United States moved toward developing a black social gospel movement.

Black church ministers drew on the tradition of abolitionist Christianity and asked, "What would a new abolition now be?" According to Union Theological Seminary professor Gary Dorrien, who has written a two-volume series on the black social gospel, "Abolitionism had come and gone. The Civil War had come and gone. Now Reconstruction had come and gone, and now they had to ask, 'What would an abolitionist tradition mean now? Because we're in as terrible a crisis as we ever were. Everything that we dreamed of has already come and gone, and yet look where we are.'"[31]

It is the black social gospel that led directly to Rev. Dr. Martin Luther King Jr. and the civil rights movement. "First, many people talk about the civil rights movement as though religion is secondary, just an undercurrent," Dorrien said in an interview. "There are ways of telling the story, and they got into the public school textbooks and the media, as though it's basically a political movement. That is just not true. I mean, the Southern Christian Leadership Conference leaders were ministers. They're every-week preachers, and the gospel is foundational for them. King couldn't have been clearer or more emphatic about what was holding him in his struggle and helping him to go on. It's not some political goal. It's the gospel."[32]

One reason Dorrien wrote a two-volume set of books on the black social gospel is because "it corrects a secularizing way of telling this story, but then it also flips it to another way, with a strong social justice aspect. It's not this comfortable, nice, church world, 'Oh, we're just trying to be nice' kind of 'Christianity.' No, that is not it either. The King that some young people have heard about all their lives is the plaster saint who was a noble idealist. Correcting that has become part of our business as well—just saying, 'No, this is what this movement really was and still is.' It's [also now] the Moral Mondays movement. It's Rev. [William] Barber. He's straight out of this."[33]

Why do we think of religion in terms of whiteness? Racism, yes. But also because the dominant narrative of Christianity as a conservative movement is irreconcilable when we see the civil rights movement as a religious movement as well. Civil rights and social activism—for the dominant conservative Christian narrative—are the province of the "secular left." When such dismissive labels are created, the religiosity of Rev. Dr. King is actively discarded. Meanwhile, in largely secular spaces on the left, we see another layer of ambivalence about religion that doesn't herald the Rev. Dr. King as a religious figure for fear of associating a movement of justice with fundamentalist religion or "backward religious types."

It's simply impossible to study Dr. King and omit the "Reverend" from his title. His doctorate was not in public policy or critical race theory, but in systematic theology. At fifteen he went to college at Morehouse, then he went to seminary, then he completed his doctorate at Boston University. He was born a preacher's kid, pursued the ministry from an early age, and was assassinated as a preacher. The civil rights movement as a whole was fueled by the black church and led by the Southern Christian Leadership Conference, a minister-led organization. The civil rights movement wasn't just the most consequential *activism* of the twentieth century in the United States; it was the most important *religious* movement. And Rev. Dr. King is the most influential clergyperson in American history.

> It's simply impossible to study Dr. King and omit the "Reverend" from his title. His doctorate was not in public policy or critical race theory, but in systematic theology.

On one hand, Americans downplay King's religiosity; on the other we de-radicalize him. In our public imagination, he and the entire civil rights movement are often reduced to the person who taught white people and black people to get along nicely. King was a radical and a religious radical who rooted his "extremism" in the fullest realization of following Jesus Christ.

Rev. Dr. King's "Letter from a Birmingham Jail" is a sacred text just like the Pauline Epistles for progressive Christians. In his letter, he expresses that his greatest disappointment lies not with the explicit racist KKK member, but rather with the moderate white Southerners who hold back social progress. And King makes a theological justification against moderation:

Though I was initially disappointed at being categorized as an extremist, as I continued to think about the matter I gradually gained a measure of satisfaction from the label. Was not Jesus an extremist for love: "Love your enemies, bless them that curse you, do good to them that hate you, and pray for them which despitefully use you, and persecute you." Was not Amos an extremist for justice: "Let justice roll down like waters and righteousness like an ever flowing stream." Was not Paul an extremist for the Christian gospel: "I bear in my body the marks of the Lord Jesus." Was not Martin Luther an extremist: "Here I stand; I cannot do otherwise, so help me God."[34]

To some, "extremist" can be a slur, but the degree of devotion to our causes isn't the problem. It's the righteousness of the cause that itself determines the degree of our devotion to the cause. The nature of Jesus Christ as revealed in the Gospels is never a moderate one. Every chance Jesus has to draw a stark line to show what the kin-dom of God looks like, he takes the chance. Jesus tells people to leave behind their families and their entire lives to follow him. While many moderate Christians have made excuses in defense of their moderation, they are hard-pressed to find in the Gospels an example of Jesus saying, "I believe in this cause, but only so far as to cost me little or nothing." King rightly places the civil rights movement in the long line of extremism for bringing about the kin-dom of God on earth as it is heaven.

"Good Teacher, what must I do to inherit eternal life?" a rich young ruler asked Jesus (Mark 10:17). Many conservative Christians offer an easy answer for that question, claiming that obtaining eternal life is about "right belief." But Jesus's answer is an extreme upending of a moderate way of life. "You lack one thing; go, sell what you own, and give the money to the poor, and you will have treasure in heaven; then come, follow me" (Mark 10:21). The idea of selling everything he owned to follow Jesus upset the man because "he had many possessions," the Gospel writer tells us (Mark 10:22). This story provides a clue to what the early Jesus movement was encountering: people resisted Jesus's extremist message of love, justice, and peace. They didn't want to upset the status quo. After the rich young ruler leaves, Jesus startles his disciples with this comment: "How hard it will be for those who have wealth to enter the kingdom of God!" (Mark 10:23).

There is no more radical message than this. Jesus tells his own followers—or his "base," as we might say today—that they need to give up everything or they are not truly following him. In the Acts of the Apostles, the writer Luke gives us a similar message in the story of two early followers, Ananias and Sapphira. They sold a piece of their property to donate the money to the movement, but they didn't give *all* of the money from the sale. The leader of the movement, Peter, responds with harsh words "Ananias, why has Satan filled your heart to lie to the Holy Spirit and to keep back part of the proceeds of the land? While it remained unsold, did it not remain your own? And after it was sold, were not the proceeds at your disposal? How is it that you have contrived this deed in your heart? You did not lie to us but to God!" (Acts 5:3–4). Hearing this, Ananias falls down and dies. Sapphira quickly meets the same fate. To de-radicalize the story, to make it anything other than extreme, is to reduce the clear message of the early church.

Rev. Dr. King's radical message echoes that of Jesus and the movement that followed him. This was the radical love and embodiment of the "Beloved Community" that Rev. Dr. King called the South and the entire nation to embrace. "Jesus Christ was an extremist for love, truth and goodness, and thereby rose above his environment," he wrote. "Perhaps the South, the nation and the world are in dire need of creative extremists."[35]

Not only was the civil rights movement one of the most important progressive religious movements in American history; it also brought about a negative and destructive reaction from conservative Christians. As the civil rights movement advanced, conservative Christians organized against what they viewed as "government overreach," which for them meant the weakening of white supremacy.

Many political observers today portray abortion as the main issue that gave conservative Christians the impetus to organize in the 1960s and 1970s, but that's a severe rewriting of history and covers up the real story of how a reactionary movement against the civil rights movement provided the fuel for the religious right.

The Supreme Court's decision in *Brown v. Board of Education* in 1954 was heralded by progressive Christians and many other Americans as a huge advance for social justice, but it didn't satisfy conservative Christians. By the 1960s, conservative

Christians started opening segregation academies, private schools in the South opened by white parents to avoid desegregated public schools like Jerry Falwell's Lynchburg Christian Academy. It was a move by conservative Christians to keep their children "pure" and away from black students, progressives, and those who taught the "anti-God" science of evolution.

Randall Balmer, a historian studying the origins of the conservative Christians' rise in the United States, points to 1969 as a turning point. In May of that year, a group of black parents in Holmes County, Mississippi, sued the Treasury Department to stop three segregation academies from obtaining tax-exempt status. In 1970 President Richard Nixon ordered the Internal Revenue Service to adopt a new policy denying segregation academies tax-exempt status, and a federal court upheld the decision in 1971. Bob Jones University didn't drop its ban on interracial dating until 2000 and didn't regain its tax-exempt status until 2017. Bob Jones University administrator Elmer L. Rumminger told Balmer in an interview for *POLITICO Magazine* that the IRS actions "alerted the Christian school community about what could happen with government interference . . . That was really the major issue that got us all involved."[36]

While explicit racism on the part of conservative Christian leaders came in reaction to the civil rights movement, a less noticed but perhaps even more influential change was the racism of white Americans who fled cities rather than have their children go to school with black children. The "white flight" that built suburban America was also the societal change that built the evangelical megachurch movement. In the "safe" confines of their all-white neighborhoods and schools, what became known as "evangelicalism" began to build its empire. The megachurch flashy lights obscured the fact that these were churches created as anti-black, conservative suburban retreats.

The religious conservatives' opposition to the civil rights nature of Rev. Dr. King's ministry also came into focus during the final years of his life, when he embraced a broader set of issues beyond the civil rights movement's priorities. Many of his fellow civil rights activists abandoned his efforts, thinking they were harmful, a kind of "mission creep" beyond civil rights. One of the most controversial speeches of King's entire ministry came not in the South nor about the treatment of black Americans, but at Riverside Church in New York City as he spoke out against the Vietnam War:

> As if the weight of such a commitment to the life and health of America were not enough, another burden of responsibility was placed upon me in 1954. And I cannot forget that the Nobel Peace Prize was also a commission, a commission to work harder than I had ever worked before for the brotherhood of man. This is a calling that takes me beyond national allegiances.
>
> But even if it were not present, I would yet have to live with the meaning of my commitment to the ministry of Jesus Christ. To me, the relationship of this ministry to the making of peace is so obvious that I sometimes marvel at those who ask me why I am speaking against the war. Could it be that they do not know that the Good

News was meant for all men—for communist and capitalist, for their children and ours, for black and for white, for revolutionary and conservative? Have they forgotten that my ministry is in obedience to the one who loved his enemies so fully that he died for them? What then can I say to the Vietcong or to Castro or to Mao as a faithful minister of this one? Can I threaten them with death or must I not share with them my life?[37]

King's commitment to respecting the God-given dignity of human life transcended national borders. King's opposition to the Vietnam War was rooted not just in the Universal Declaration of Human Rights (adopted by the United Nations in 1948) but in his identity as a follower of Jesus. His Christian commitment to not valuing American lives or the interests of the United States over people's lives in other countries was just as radical an idea as the commitment to racial justice that King advocated for in the United States.

King was willing to prophetically critique people he partnered with on some issues when they disagreed and was unafraid to keep pushing once he made some gains. He partnered closely with the President of the United States, Lyndon Baines Johnson, to pass civil rights legislation. But that didn't cement King's allegiance to LBJ, as his allegiance always remained to the ministry of Jesus Christ. King's critique of LBJ and the Vietnam War lost him much of the popular support he had gained from the civil rights movement. In retrospect, he looks even more like a prophet for making the case.

After King's assassination, his wife and partner in the struggle for freedom, Coretta Scott King, continued to prophetically push forward the work of collective liberation by advocating for LGBTQ rights. When she invited black poet and lesbian Audre Lorde to speak at the twentieth anniversary of the March on Washington, Lorde had this to say:

> I am Audre Lorde, speaking for the National Coalition of Black Gays. Today's march openly joins the black civil rights movement and the gay civil rights movement in the struggles we have always shared, the struggle for jobs, for health, for peace and for freedom. We marched in 1963 with Dr. Martin Luther King and dared to dream that freedom would include us, because not one of us is free to choose the terms of our living until all of us are free to choose the terms of our living.[38]

Coretta Scott King also spoke at Human Rights Campaign events to express her "solidarity with the gay and lesbian movement."[39] In 2004, when President George W. Bush made a constitutional amendment banning same-sex marriage part of his appeal to conservatives, Scott King spoke out: "A constitutional amendment banning same-sex marriage is a form of gay bashing and it would do nothing to protect traditional marriages."[40]

Religious radicals, the Kings spent their entire lives pushing for equality and dignity, most prominently for black Americans, but also for the LGBTQ community, for people in other countries who were the victims of the US military-industrial complex, and for the poor.

Emphasizing the Christian-ness of Rev. Dr. King is not an attempt to exert Christian supremacy against other people of faith or people of no faith. It's a corrective to the secularization of the civil rights movement and black political activism that continues today. We can see in King's own activism the religious pluralism he championed. King partnered closely with people of other faiths and modeled interfaith alliance building. One of the most famous examples is the active involvement of Rabbi Abraham Joshua Heschel. Arm-in-arm with John Lewis, Rev. King, and other ministers, Heschel crossed the Selma bridge.

The Polish-American Rabbi Heschel escaped Poland weeks before the Nazi invasion in 1939 and moved to the United States in 1940. His mother and three of his four sisters died in the Holocaust. Inspired by his study of the Hebrew prophets, Rabbi Heschel's activism in the civil rights movement makes him a hero to many Jewish social justice activists today. He later joined Dr. King in opposing the Vietnam War.

King drew inspiration from Gandhian Hinduism for his emphasis on nonviolence. "To other countries I may go as a tourist, but to India I come as a pilgrim," King said during his visit there in 1959.[41] "I came to see for the first time that the Christian doctrine of love operating through the Gandhian method of nonviolence was one of the most potent weapons available to oppressed people in their struggle for freedom," he later wrote about his trip.[42]

King modeled a Christian commitment to interfaith activism that continues to inspire activists today. It's perhaps most evident in the work of Rev. Dr. William Barber II, who has taken up the mantle of the Poor People's Campaign and revived it fifty years after King launched his campaign. Like Rev. Dr. King before him, Rev. Dr. Barber connects the evils of militarism, racism, and poverty to the causes of oppression, and like King, Barber remains deeply rooted in his Christian identity. He also follows King in the tradition of strong multi-faith alliances across Jewish, Muslim, and other religious identities.

During the speech at Riverside Church about the Vietnam War, King called for a "radical revolution of values."[43] It's a revolution we still yearn for and need in the world today. For progressive Christians like King, it's a revolution rooted not in some vague "progressive values" or a generic equality, but in the gospel message Jesus Christ proclaimed. The radical revolution of values is rooted in God's love that we are called to share with others, and its flowers are peace and human dignity. Following King's lead, we join in common cause with people of shared faith, other faiths, and no faith who champion the same values.

CHAPTER 4

SWORDS INTO PLOWSHARES

When Rev. Dr. King called for a "radical revolution of values" at Riverside Church,[44] his words came in direct response to the war in Vietnam, though they are applicable to all wars. God does not just care about American lives, but about the lives of all people on earth. War is an affront to the image of God in all people. Whether you're a pacifist Christian who believes war is always wrong or someone who believes in the possibility of "just war," the loss of life associated with war is always lamentable. From the Vietnam War era to today, the peace movement has always been a major part of the progressive movement in the United States. Today's Christian peace movement draws on a long history of activism that goes back to Jesus's own ministry. By the 1960s, progressive Christians were on the front lines of opposition to the war in Vietnam and in later decades participated in the nuclear disarmament.

Rev. Dr. King's opposition to the Vietnam War was a significant moment in a much larger organizing initiative known as the National Emergency Committee of Clergy and Laymen Concerned about Vietnam. In his book *Because of Their Faith: CALCAV and Religious Opposition to the Vietnam War*, historian Mitchell Hall documents the early and consistent opposition from religious leaders to the Vietnam War.[45]

One of the most fascinating aspects of the anti-war movement was that its leadership included mainline Protestant, Catholic, and Jewish leaders. Faith leaders like Rabbi Abraham Joshua Heschel and Rev. Dr. King, as well as William Sloane Coffin, and the Catholic activist brothers Daniel and Philip Berrigan shared a common commitment to prophetic resistance.

Isaiah 2:4 became a rallying cry for peace activists: "He shall judge between the nations, and shall arbitrate for many peoples; they shall beat their swords into plowshares, and their spears into pruning hooks; nation shall not lift up sword against nation, neither shall they learn war any more."

On the Catholic side of progressive Christian activism, Daniel and Philip Berrigan became national newsmakers for their resistance to the American war machine during the Vietnam era and onward. The Berrigans first became national heroes to the progressive movement as part of the "Catonsville Nine." On May 17, 1968, they "walked into a draft board in Catonsville, Maryland, . . . removed draft files of young men who were about to be sent to Vietnam, . . . carted the files outside and burned them in two garbage cans with homemade napalm."[46]

"They went underground, and for a time two priests were among the criminals most wanted by the Federal Bureau of

Investigation."[47] Eventually, they were arrested and spent time in jail, but their incarceration did not deter them from their sacred resistance. On September 9, 1980, they made national headlines again for being part of "the Plowshares eight," entering the General Electric Nuclear Missile Re-entry Division in King of Prussia, Pennsylvania, and used hammers to smash two nuclear missile nose cones to bring Isaiah's prophetic words to life.[48]

In an interview in 2008 to mark forty years since the Catonsville act of sacred resistance, Daniel Berrigan said, "It is very rare to sustain a movement in recognizable form without a spiritual base." He kept his peace activism going from Vietnam, through the nuclear disarmament movement, and into the twenty-first-century opposition to the War on Terror. After all of these battles, he told *The Nation*, "I have never had such meager expectations of the system,"[49] Philip died in 2002 and Daniel in 2016.

On the Protestant side of Christian activism, William Sloane Coffin was active in Vietnam-era protests and then the nuclear disarmament movement as senior minister of the Riverside Church from 1977 to 1987. Coffin stuck with the liberal theological tradition, once preaching, "It is bad religion to deify doctrines and creeds. . . . Doctrines, let's not forget, supported slavery and apartheid. . . . Moreover, doctrines can divide while compassion can only unite."[50]

But he also pushed the tradition forward in embracing a global movement for peace and reassessing the role of the United States in the world. "No sermon on love can fail to mention love's most difficult problem in our time—how to find effective ways to alleviate the massive suffering of humanity at home and abroad," Coffin preached. "What we need to realize is that to love effectively we must act collectively."[51]

Oftentimes, when we think about peace activists it's a secularized "hippie" picture. The Berrigans, Coffin, and other Christian peace activists showed the country that militarism was incompatible with following Jesus.

Anti-war activism by Christians continues to this day but, sadly, is overshadowed by the pro-war views of Christians today. While prophetic Christians followed Jesus and supported the cause of peace, conservative Christians have more and more turned toward worshipping militarism and nationalism.

One date that stands out in particular was the National Association of Evangelicals' 1983 conference in Orlando, Florida, when President Ronald Reagan gave his "Evil Empire" speech attacking the Soviet Union and contrasting it with the Christian morality of the United States. This was a major turning point in associating liberalism with "Godless" communism as a mechanism of advancing the Cold War era and "America First" thinking. Conservative Christians not only ignored the call of the Gospels and the Hebrew prophets to be peacemakers; they actively supported the American empire's use of military force.

My First Cause as a Progressive Christian

My own introduction to this bold tradition came with the United States' illegal and immoral invasion of Iraq. At the time, I was thirteen years old, and this had a profound impact on the development of my faith.

Imagine the rude awakening I had when, having grown up in a liberal Methodist church, I realized that George W. Bush and Dick Cheney were also United Methodists. The invasion of Iraq awakened my religious motivations and my political engagement. I preached a sermon on "Youth Sunday" in 2006 while in high school and focused on the need for Christians to love our enemies. I couldn't understand why our country, led by two Methodists, was bombing our enemies instead of praying for them. It was a simplistic understanding of war and peace perhaps, but there is a fundamental disconnect between the tough-talking bombing campaign during the Invasion of Iraq dubbed "shock and awe" and following Jesus.

The president of the United Methodist Church's Council of Bishops—as close as the UMC has to a pope—wrote to President Bush to plead with him for peace and to not launch the war.

Bishop Sharon Brown Christopher of southern Illinois wrote, "We pray that every possible means to prevent war will be pursued in the coming days. This is not a moment for haste but rather for deep thoughtfulness and prayer. It is a moment to reflect upon the well-spoken concerns of our allies around the world. The welfare of our human family depends on it."[52]

There was also a concerted effort from the Vatican to stop the invasion. A letter from Pope John Paul II that was only declassified by the US government in 2019 reads: "I have spared no effort in asking all parties to take every measure to ensure that the precious gift of peace is preserved and protected. I am convinced that peace is always possible even in the most difficult situations."[53]

As these events unfolded, my activism grew. The same year I delivered the sermon, I won a scholarship to attend a week-long peace activist training in Washington, DC, where I began to learn peaceful resistance from Quakers. They, along with the other historic peace churches—the Amish, Mennonites, and Church of the Brethren—have the longest and most committed stance as advocates for strict pacifism, and resisting any efforts to make their members fight in war. Quaker-led peace efforts continue today with the American Friends Service Committee and the Friends Committee on National Legislation being two of the strongest faith-based advocates for peace.

For many progressives, myself among them, the peace-church strain is a foundational part of our identity. In the Quaker training we looked at Luke 6:27–36, where Jesus says:

> But I say to you that listen, Love your enemies, do good to those who hate you, bless those who curse you, pray for those who abuse you. If anyone strikes you on the cheek, offer the other also; and from anyone who takes away your coat do not withhold even your shirt. Give to everyone who begs from you; and if anyone takes away your goods, do not ask for them again. Do to others as you would have them do to you.
>
> If you love those who love you, what credit is that to you? For even sinners love those who love them. If

you do good to those who do good to you, what credit is that to you? For even sinners do the same. If you lend to those from whom you hope to receive, what credit is that to you? Even sinners lend to sinners, to receive as much again. But love your enemies, do good, and lend, expecting nothing in return. Your reward will be great, and you will be children of the Most High; for he is kind to the ungrateful and the wicked. Be merciful, just as your Father is merciful.

As academic, activist, and author Cornel West says, "Justice is what love looks like in public."[54] The foreign affairs corollary to that sentiment might be "The peace movement is what love looks like in a world of endless war."

When it came to the US invasion of Iraq, President Bush and Vice President Cheney lost the support of the leadership of their own United Methodist Church, but were able to count on the much more conservative Southern Baptist Convention to support their agenda. Richard Land, president of the Ethics and Religious Liberty Commission of the Southern Baptist Convention and a key backer of the Iraq War, said this about then–Secretary of State Colin Powell's appearance before the United Nations: "The case for using force to bring about

> As Cornel West says, "Justice is what love looks like in public." The foreign affairs corollary to that sentiment might be "The peace movement is what love looks like in a world of endless war."

disarmament and regime change in Iraq was clearly and convincingly made for anyone who has eyes to see and ears to hear. Our choice is to pay less now and deal with this problem or we can pay a lot more later and deal with a nuclear-armed Saddam."[55]

Pacifism and Just War Theory

Progressive Christians have had held differences of opinion about supporting war, and it's important to note those differences. Some progressives are strict pacifists. They take the Christian commitment to nonviolence to the extreme by opposing the use of armed forces in all circumstances. Others, influenced by Catholic social teaching, hold to an understanding of "just war theory." Even as they believe there are very few wars that can be considered just (in the sense of the right thing to do) from a moral standpoint, they believe there are both just reasons to launch a military intervention and just ways of conducting war.

Just war theory holds to certain criteria for going to war: necessitated by a just cause, recognized by a competent authority, the right intention, probability of success, and a proportional response to the incident that led to the war. For some progressives, just causes for war have been shaped by believing in the Responsibility to Protect, a 2005 United Nations global political commitment to protect populations from mass-atrocity crimes. I include myself in this generation of progressives. Following the Rwandan genocide and after reading *A Problem from Hell: America in the Age of Genocide* by Samantha Power,[56] who would later become President Obama's Ambassador to the United Nations, I began to believe that the world community has a responsibility to protect the most vulnerable from genocide. Any American military engagement for limited humanitarian causes must be recognized by the authority of the United Nations Security Council and the United States Congress.

But within the spectrum of progressive Christian understanding about just war or strict pacifism, progressives meet in agreement that the United States' endless wars in the Middle East are unjust, just as the Vietnam War was in an earlier time. Today what's missing, unlike in the Vietnam era, is a mobilized progressive Christian anti-war movement. While there are valiant efforts today, the weakness of the movement is evident in not being able to pressure President Obama to follow through on his vow to end the wars in Iraq and Afghanistan.

It's incumbent on progressive Christians like us to wake ourselves up from accepting infinite military engagement abroad. How long must wars in the Middle East drag on? As social justice issues on other subjects come and go from the national spotlight, we've all seemingly accepted the fact that endless war is a fact of life. It's not. With all the concerns progressive Christians in the United States have about domestic policies, it can be difficult to focus on intractable foreign entanglements. The call for peace and justice must be global for Christians because we do not worship an American God. And, as we will see in the next chapter, foreign affairs and domestic affairs are not easily separated categories.

CHAPTER 5

GOD'S LOVE HAS NO BORDERS

The progressive Christian belief that all people have value, not just Americans, serves as inspiration for both peace activism and our treatment of newcomers to the United States. There is no distinction between the God-given dignity of American citizens and the God-given dignity of citizens of other nations. The issues of war and US foreign policy are inextricably linked to the issue of immigration, as political instability is a leading cause of people leaving their countries of origin. The influx of refugees and immigrants from Latin America is in large part due to the destructive role the United States has played in the region.

This harm perpetrated by the United States in Latin America is something I learned about at an early age from my grandmother, Frances Bell Graves. She traveled extensively throughout Latin America as a missionary who cared deeply about social justice. She volunteered with Witness for Peace, a faith-based organization that began in 1983 in opposition to the Reagan administration's support of the Nicaraguan Contras. She traveled with them to provide protective accompaniment to the Nicaraguan people caught in war zones. She learned about the conflict in Nicaragua from Henri Nouwen, the Dutch Catholic priest, who gave a talk about his experience there. "I took my notebook but I was so impressed by what he said that I looked at my notebook later and I hadn't taken any notes, but I was crying because it was such a sad situation in Nicaragua," she told me.[57]

Witness for Peace had a strategy of Americans going to the places where the Contras, funded by the Reagan/Bush administration, were killing Sandinistas. The Americans who filled that protective role were given the name "Shield of Love" because, as my grandmother said, "as long as they were in a village, that village would not be attacked."[58] In 1985, a Witness for Peace delegation was kidnapped by the Contras and held in captivity for three days—an event that sparked media coverage in the United States and brought congressional attention to the evil happening in Nicaragua, funded by the US government.

The Sanctuary Movement: Then and Now

Christians in the United States like my grandmother were moved to action by crises in Central America during the 1980s—including many Catholic sisters. Similar to today's migration in light of political turmoil, refugees fled civil wars and political repression in Central America and sought out safety in the United States. The migrants from Central America fled through Mexico to escape brutal governments in their own countries.

On March 24, 1982, the Sanctuary Movement was officially born with six congregations in Arizona and California declaring themselves "sanctuaries." They began offering their church buildings to assist the Central Americans who came to the United States without proper authorization. These Christians committed to the radical inclusion of all people. These congregations were also persecuted by the US government. The Immigration and Naturalization Service (a precursor to Immigration and Customs Enforcement, or ICE) used informants to infiltrate the Sanctuary Movement and indicted sixteen movement leaders, including clergy, for breaking the law. Eight were convicted, but all were given probation for their "crimes."[59]

More than five hundred congregations declared themselves "sanctuaries" during the 1980s, struggling to welcome Central American asylum seekers.[60] Sanctuary Movement leaders looked to one of the central questions in the Gospels: "Who is my neighbor?" This is a question posed to Jesus by an "expert in the law." Jesus responds by telling the parable of the Good Samaritan, a parable that has shaped progressive Christianity for two thousand years. "Who was a neighbor?" Jesus asks the expert in the law. "The one who had mercy on him," is the answer he receives. Jesus then tells "the expert" to "go and do likewise." Today, churches across the country continue to act on the mandate of mercy, to "go and do likewise" (Luke 10:25–37).

Migrants coming to the United States have always forced us to ask this question as Americans. Now, as the flow of Central American migrants fleeing government persecution continues, individuals draw on the bold history of the Sanctuary Movement of the 1980s. The New Sanctuary Movement that launched in the mid-2000s points to showing mercy and compassion to migrants coming to the United States.

Progressive people of faith have been especially galvanized by the Trump administration's attacks on immigration policies. More than one thousand churches and other houses of worship have become sanctuaries, according to Church World Service, a cooperative ministry of thirty-seven Christian (primarily Protestant) denominations.[61]

As with earlier Sanctuary Movement leaders, the US government has gone after faith-based immigration activists like Scott Warren, a volunteer with No More Deaths, a ministry of the Unitarian Universalist Church in Tucson, Arizona. He was arrested by ICE for aiding undocumented immigrants crossing our southern border and was prosecuted for criminal conspiracy. Thankfully, he was found not guilty.[62]

Rev. Kaji Douša, co-chair of the New Sanctuary Coalition and senior pastor of Park Avenue Christian Church in New York City, had been ministering with members of a "migrant caravan" from Central America in Tijuana in 2019, when she was stopped for questioning as she was on her way back into the United States. She later discovered that she had been placed on a secret government watch list targeting immigration activists. Both Pastor Kaji

Douša and Scott Warren have argued that their right to freely practice their religious beliefs is being threatened by the Trump administration.

In May 2014, a delegation of Catholic bishops and Cardinal Sean O'Malley conducted a "Border Mass" that included serving communion through the border fence to people on the other side. As part of two days of organized visits to groups working on the border and meeting with Department of Homeland Security officials, the group went out into the desert to get a sense of the hardships faced by migrants who journey into our country for the hope of a better life.

I accompanied the bishops on the trip because I was working at the time as the Faith Coordinator at the National Immigration Forum. As I walked in the desert among the group of delegates, we discovered backpacks and other signs of human life amid the arid landscape, in seemingly unbearable conditions. Meeting activists who work to bring lifesaving humanitarian aid to migrants in these conditions is the most inspiring experience I've ever had.

Most commentary on immigration happens from the safe confines of cable news studios in New

> Most commentary on immigration happens from the safe confines of cable news studios in New York City. But for those who work at the border, abstract discussions about "the rule of law" and "getting in line" become moot, in light of the conditions people face in order to come to the United States.

York City. But for those who work at the border, abstract discussions about "the rule of law" and "getting in line" become moot, in light of the conditions people face in order to come to the United States. For those working with migrants, there's little doubt that if New York media and viewers witnessed the truth of the migrant experience, they'd recognize that opening our doors to welcome them is truly a just response.

Many migrants have done more to realize the promise of life, liberty, and the pursuit of happiness than native-born Americans could ever imagine. They are teaching us to understand the weight and grace of answering the mandate to love our neighbor, and teaching us to welcome those arriving from Central America as though we are welcoming Christ himself.

CHAPTER 6

FROM SENECA FALLS TO SELMA
TO STONEWALL

We, the people, declare today that the most evident of truths, that all of us are created equal, is the star that guides us still, just as it guided our forebears through to Seneca Falls and Selma and Stonewall, just as it guided all those men and women, sung and unsung, who left footprints along this great Mall to hear a preacher say that we cannot walk alone, to hear a King proclaim that our individual freedom is inextricably bound to the freedom of every soul on Earth.

—President Barack Obama's Second Inaugural
Address (January 21, 2013)

President Obama's connection of the long struggle for human rights—from the women's rights convention at Seneca Falls, to the march for civil rights in Selma, to the Stonewall riots that marked a major turning point in LGBTQ rights history—isn't just alliteration; it's the path marking the history of the progressive movement. Every step on the path was charted, in part, by Christian activists like President Obama himself. In chapter 3 we looked at the religious motivations of the civil rights movement. People familiar with religious motivation for progressive causes often point to the civil rights movement. Given the dominance the religious right has in shaping our current understanding of faith and politics, two of the most erased religious aspects of the modern progressive movements are the struggle for LGBTQ rights and the struggle for women's reproductive rights.

From the Very Beginning of the LGBTQ Rights Movement

You might expect me, as a gay man, to be the most familiar with the LGBTQ part of this story. But I stumbled upon a big part of this history quite by chance. Attending seminary in New York City meant, for me, quite a few trips on the 1 train downtown to the Village.

One morning during my final year of seminary, I walked past the Church of the Village. It's part of the United Methodist Church, and known as one of the most progressive churches in the city. Even though I was in the process of leaving the UMC over its anti-LGBTQ policy, I still had a strong emotional reaction every time I passed a local church. I still do. Each of the Methodist communities I was involved with made a huge impact on who

I am today—and I continue to be grateful for their ongoing ministry. But like many, I didn't love the United Methodist Church's ban on ordaining and marrying LGBTQ members. While some churches and regional bodies of the UMC openly defy this ban, it's been on the church's law books since 1972. Suffice it to say, I experience an upswell of emotional baggage when passing a Methodist church.

On this particular morning, while walking through the Village, I saw a plaque on the wall of the Church of the Village that faced the busy NYC street. It was a city historical marker noting that the church was the original meeting place of Parents and Friends of Lesbians and Gays (PFLAG) on March 11, 1973. As I saw the sign, in Methodist terminology, my heart was "strangely warmed."

While the institutional, global church debated the dignity of all people through official church law, this particular group of followers of Jesus in the Wesleyan tradition had been on the front lines of what became the LGBTQ rights movement. Seeing the sign reminded me of one of the things I love most about John Wesley, the founder of Methodism. Wesley combined a zeal for preaching the gospel with a strong commitment to social justice that included opposing slavery and supporting the ordination of women.

PFLAG wasn't the only early LGBTQ rights movement that had a Christian link in Lower Manhattan. From the very beginning of the Stonewall riots, churches stepped up and joined the protests. The Church of the Holy Apostles in Chelsea, part of the Episcopal Church, was from 1969 to 1974 "one of the most important meeting places in New York City for organizations of the early post-Stonewall gay rights movement, including the West Side Discussion Group, Gay Liberation Front, and Gay Activists Alliance," according to the NYC LGBT Historic Sites Project.[63] On the West Coast, Glide Memorial United Methodist in San Francisco's Tenderloin district got involved in the LGBTQ rights movement, even before Stonewall. Cecil Williams and Ted McIllvenna, both Methodist ministers, spoke out on January 2, 1965, about San Francisco unjustly targeting the LGBTQ community.[64]

This is obviously not part of the dominant narrative of Christianity in the United States. While there's much to be proud of in the long history of progressive Christian activism, any random person on the street could tell you that "Christian" today does not bring to mind solidarity with the Stonewall Riots and crusading for human rights.

I've been living and breathing progressive Christianity since long before I sat down to write this book, yet even I was surprised to learn about the Christian support for the very early LGBTQ rights movement. I've found that my experience is not unique. Many progressive Christians have an internalized association of Christianity with conservatism—even if we know it's not true. While we're trying our best to follow Jesus, we're constantly inundated with a culture that tells us something very different about our faith.

We've all had experiences when we mention we're Christians and people look at us like we're crazy to associate ourselves with conservatives. My second notable Village experience speaks to this. I was a few blocks away from the Church of the Village at a queer dive bar with a non-churchy gay friend. I had recently started seminary, and thus could no longer avoid bringing up my faith in non-churchy social situations. Some single friends in seminary would just say they were in "grad school" to avoid people's questions or immediately associating "seminary" with social conservatism.

I bit the bullet and decided to be open about being in seminary with the strangers we met at the bar. Their faces registered shock, just as mine did on seeing the plaque outside the Church of the Village. I'm assuming some red flags were immediately raised. Was I a self-hating gay man who tortured himself with religion? Was I even gay at all, or was I trying to infiltrate a gay bar with my hate? My point is, talking about my faith in a gay bar didn't immediately bring up the memories of churches supporting the early LGBTQ rights movement—even though we were quite literally surrounded by many churches that then were— and now are—supportive of our freedom.

Christian Support for Reproductive Justice before and Possibly after Roe v. Wade

Another major issue of today's progressive movement that has been secularized is the movement for reproductive rights. The religious case for making abortion safe and legal has been erased from our public discourse.

Christian feminists have long struggled for equality within the church and in society as a whole. The tradition includes lifelong United Methodist Hillary Clinton's famous proclamation at the 1995 UN Fourth World Conference on Women in Beijing that "women's rights are human rights and human rights are women's rights." Clinton's Christian motivation in her advocacy for women's rights is rarely mentioned. Similarly, we all learn in school about the Seneca Falls Convention that paved the way for women's right to vote, but we forget that that conference took place at the Wesleyan Methodist Church in Seneca Falls. Many members of the women's rights movement in the United States have been and continue to be inspired by their faith.

Talking about women's rights can be a conversation stopper when making the case for reclaiming progressive Christianity. During an open discussion I helped facilitate in New Orleans in 2018 at the Religious Left Caucus at Netroots Nation, the largest gathering of progressive activists in the country, one older woman looked at me and said with a lot of pain in her voice, "What do you say when conservatives just respond to anything you say by accusing you of killing babies?" It's a question every progressive Christian of any gender encounters today when we try to engage the public square with our faith. And there's often a tendency to recoil, talk about "choice" as a way to avoid the topic of abortion, or otherwise look away. No other issue more greatly embodies the "secular left vs. religious right" argument today than abortion. But like every progressive social movement, the movement for reproductive justice has a bold tradition of Christian activism.

Religious activists in the movement aimed to liberalize abortion laws so that women—especially women of color—could have safe access to medical services, which would prevent the deaths of women who sought out unsafe means. To that end Howard Moody, the senior minister of Judson Memorial Church in New York City, helped to start the Clergy Consultation Service (CCS) in 1967.

"In woman's age-long struggle for first-class citizenship and genuine equality in the personhood of the human race, one of the last and most formidable barriers for her is in this area of reproductive rights—the personal and private freedom to determine when and how her reproductive organs will function," Moody and Arlene Carmen of Judson wrote in their book about their activism.[65] "That fundamental right is now in most of the states abridged by restrictive abortion statutes." Initially a group of twenty-one Protestant and Jewish religious leaders, by 1973 the CCS had roughly 1,400 clergy members across the country joining the cause of helping women obtain safe abortions.

In a recent article about the current abortion laws debate, Bridgette Dunlap wrote in the *Atlantic* that Moody and Carmen's book is "a surprising read today." Because it was "written before religious opposition to abortion was widespread, Moody and Carmen spend few words on the morality of abortion; they treat the pastoral obligation to help women access safe, affordable abortions almost as a given. Instead, they focus on the practical realities for women in need of dignified abortion care, offering insights into how the service should be delivered to best serve patients that contrast sharply with today's trend toward laws mandating overly medicalized abortion procedures."[66]

After the 1973 *Roe v. Wade* decision, the progressive Christian leadership in advancing women's reproductive health care continued with the Religious Coalition for Abortion Rights. In 1993, the group changed its name to the Religious Coalition for Reproductive Choice. The Coalition now includes many mainline Protestant and Jewish groups as well as the Catholics for Choice organization.

Conservative Christians didn't participate in this type of proactive advocacy, but there also wasn't widespread opposition to abortion in mainstream evangelical thought around the time of *Roe*. Opposition and activist expression were largely driven by the Catholic hierarchy, which also opposed all forms of birth control. *Christianity Today*, the flagship magazine of evangelicalism, even issued a special issue on abortion in 1968, which, according to CNN, "[encapsulated] the consensus among evangelical thinkers at the time. In the leading article, professor Bruce Waltke, of the famously conservative Dallas Theological Seminary, explained the Bible plainly teaches that life begins at birth."[67]

It was only later that conservative Christian opposition to abortion coalesced across Protestant and Catholic lines. As racism became less palatable as an overt stance for the religious right, they looked for a new issue. Soon "purity" became the attack on liberalism/modernism/secularism that took up the causes of LGBTQ rights and women's rights.

In our public imagination today, that advocacy succeeded in equating "Christian voter" with "anti-abortion voter." But the work for reproductive justice continues with leadership from the current senior minister at Judson Memorial Church, Rev. Dr. Donna Schaper. She and progressive Christian clergy are preparing for life after *Roe v Wade* in case the conservative Supreme Court does, as some have warned, overturn the law. Today, with an unprecedented attack on women's reproductive health in Republican-controlled legislatures across the country, we could be on the precipice of abortion becoming illegal in states controlled by conservative Christians.

Rev. Dr. Schaper, who participated in the Clergy Consultation Service pre-*Roe*, said in a *Religion Dispatches* interview, "Before *Roe*, it was understood that counseling someone to have an abortion was illegal. Many clergy were picked up for it. I have a feeling that civil disobedience may be required, like the baker who won't bake cakes for same-sex couples. We may have to say, 'we will not *not* provide counseling' using a religious freedom argument."[68]

I've noticed a tendency by some progressive Christians to avoid talking about reproductive health care and instead focus on the conservative Christians' narrow focus on the subject. We should not avoid the debate or pivot to other subjects. Guaranteeing access to reproductive health care is an expression of following Jesus, who believed and trusted women.

There is common ground to find with principled Christians who believe life starts at conception, including free birth control and other pro-family progressive ideas. When we start from a place of finding common ground on not criminalizing abortion, I believe people of good faith who disagree about when life begins can unite around universal health care efforts that will have the effect of reducing the number of people who end up having abortions.

Women's rights and LGBTQ rights are two key issues in today's progressive movement. Alongside the ongoing civil rights movement for the full equality of black Americans, our country continues down the path from Seneca to Selma to Stonewall. While this path toward the full equality of all has been charted by many religious Americans, sadly, we only hear it talked about in secular terms today.

Today we are witnessing an evolution of the movement for equality for all that is pushing for unapologetic pride and a reckoning with past harms. The goals across movements are liberation and accountability for the histories of oppression faced by so many people. This bold call for justice has, unsurprisingly, led to a reaction from the right.

Conservatives and the media label this movement "identity politics" as a pejorative. The use of this term by those in our society who are content for it to be dominated by straight, rich, white men is an attempt to secularize and minimize the movement. But people of faith are again leading these movements. Our diverse identities are a gift from God, and God calls us to the work of justice, liberation, and truth. For Christians, this movement is deeply inspired and motivated by the greatest theological advance of the twentieth century: liberation theology. That's the topic we turn to in our final chapter of Part One.

CHAPTER 7

THE RELIGIOUS ROOTS OF "IDENTITY POLITICS"

There's no escaping the term "identity politics" in our political discourse today. Like "social justice warrior," this term is sometimes used as a pejorative. But at the heart of "identity politics" are various minorities in our country demanding justice and liberation from oppression. Liberation theology, which emerged simultaneously in the United States with black liberation theology and in Latin America in the Catholic Church, is the Christian tradition making that same demand for liberation from oppression.

My introduction to liberation theology was in Latin America, then it led me to Union Theological Seminary to study under the father of black liberation theology, Rev. Dr. James Cone.

I first volunteered with Amigos de las Américas, a nonprofit international youth leadership and development organization, when I was sixteen. I spent two months in a rural Panamanian village. On my last day in the community, one woman told me, "Rucuérdanos, los pobres, en la tierra de Dios." *Remember us, the poor, in the land of God.*

Her words drew a stark "us" and "them" dynamic at the heart of liberation theology. I was the privileged American who would soon return to the "land of God." She asked me to remember the poor, and I've tried my best to take that command to heart. My form of privilege as an American citizen became a responsibility to change US foreign policy in Latin America for the better. It's one of the reasons I studied international relations at American University, where President John F. Kennedy announced the creation of the Peace Corps and urged graduates to "wage peace."

My experience in Panama and later stints with Amigos de las Américas in Nicaragua and Paraguay exposed me to liberation theology for the first time in the work of Gustavo Gutiérrez. The context for Gutiérrez, a Peruvian Catholic priest, and his revolutionary theology was the Second Vatican Council, or Vatican II. Just as American Protestantism embraced modernism around the same time as the Social Gospel, the Catholic Church in Latin America evolved as it came to terms with advances brought about by the modern world through Vatican II. Pope John XXIII and Pope Paul VI convened the council between 1962 and 1965, and it led to sweeping changes in how the Catholic Church would be engaged in the world. Catholics began to pray with other Christian denominations and were encouraged to work with people of non-Christian faiths, and Masses, previously celebrated solely in Latin, began to be held in the languages of local communities. In short, the church evolved.

"Prior to this time, the church had been almost seen as a fortress, very much concerned about its own internal stability and integrity and engaging the world in terms of missionary activity," Xavier University's Peter A. Huff said about Vatican II during an NPR retrospective in 2012. "Pope John wanted to reinforce that missionary mandate, but he also wanted to create an environment of dialogue, where the church would engage in all the forces of the modern world."[69]

One way the church embraced the modern world was by listening more to voices from the developing world. Gutiérrez wrote about extreme poverty and the domination by the United States in Latin America. His theology would prove to be influential throughout the world, and he became known as the father of liberation theology in Latin America. Like the Social Gospel, liberation theology is rooted in Jesus's caring for the material needs and well-being of the most vulnerable in society. "Faith is not limited to affirming the existence of God," Gutiérrez wrote. "No, faith tells us that God loves us and demands a loving response. This response is given through love for human beings, and that is what we mean by a commitment to God and to our neighbor."[70]

As Gutiérrez looked to Gospel texts for Jesus's teachings, he also looked to the experience of the Exodus, as God freed the Israelites from exploitation under the hands of Pharaoh and delivered them to freedom. And he pointed his finger at countries like the United States, which has often acted as a modern-day Pharaoh imposing its colonialist power in the Americas. Rather,

Gutiérrez said that God called the United States to *free* the people of Latin America. For Gutiérrez, "the poor are a by-product of the system in which we live and for which we are responsible. They are marginalized by our social and cultural world. They are the oppressed, exploited proletariat, robbed of the fruit of their labor and despoiled of their humanity. Hence the poverty of the poor is not a call to generous relief action, but a demand that we go and build a different social order."[71]

Gutiérrez and liberation theology went too far for more conservative Catholic leaders and set off alarm bells at the Vatican. By the early 1980s, Pope John Paul II and his top lieutenant, Cardinal Ratzinger (who would later become Pope Benedict XVI), launched an all-out attack on liberation theology.

"This conception of Christ as a political figure, a revolutionary, as the subversive of Nazareth," Pope John Paull II said, "does not tally with the church's catechism."[72] Cardinal Ratzinger warned that liberation theology wrongly combined "the Bible's view of history with Marxist dialectics" and labeled it a "singular heresy."[73] Both church leaders saw the movement as too political and too focused on alleviating extreme poverty.

When Pope Francis became pope, the Vatican's tune changed radically. While he wasn't known as a hard-charging liberation theologian, he shared a similar focus for the church on care for the poor. As liberation theology's "preferential option for the poor" became strongly accepted by the first Latin American pope, he even invited Gutiérrez to the Vatican, giving him a warm welcome.[74]

While this strain of liberation theology had its roots in Latin America, it also had a profound effect on the United States. Many American churches became active in supporting leftists in Latin America and opposing the Reagan and Bush administrations' support for far-right dictatorships. One of the longest-standing annual faith-based protests in the United States was the School of the Americas protest in Ft. Benning, Georgia, where the US trained far-right militias from Latin America. This tradition continues today. My mom and I took a road trip to the School of the Americas protest in 2011. The theme was "Occupy Fort Benning," which drew on the ongoing Occupy movement that protested social and economic inequality around the world.

For Gutiérrez, one of the most important aspects of liberation theology is the idea that theology is a second act *after* we witness human action and experience. "A theology which has as its points of reference only 'truths' which have been established once and for all—and not the Truth which is also the Way—can only be static and, in the long run, sterile," Gutiérrez writes at the beginning of his landmark text, A *Theology*

> For Gutiérrez, one of the most important aspects of liberation theology is the idea that theology is a second act *after* we witness human action and experience. "A theology which has as its points of reference only 'truths' which have been established once and for all—and not the Truth which is also the Way—can only be static and, in the long run, sterile," Gutiérrez writes.

of Liberation, published in 1971.[75] Theology comes out of the lived experience of people and reflects on the social sciences that analyze the human condition.

The theologian had a specific role, according to Gutiérrez, as someone who "will be engaged where nations, social classes, people struggle to free themselves from domination and oppression by other nations, classes, and people."[76] This was the kind of revolutionary theological thinking of the 1970s that also reshaped US Protestant theology. And while Gutiérrez and other Latin American theologians pushed for liberation, other voices arose that reflected understandings specific to the United States, such as theologians like Rev. Dr. James Cone, who wrote out of the black American experience.

The Rev. Dr. James Cone, considered the father of black liberation theology, revolutionized progressive Christian theology. A professor at Union Theological Seminary, Cone spoke out about the great evils of racism in the United States without any attempt to moderate his views to appease the consciences of white people. Dr. Cone writes: "the demonic forces of racism are real for the black man. Theologically, Malcolm X was not far wrong when he called the white man 'the devil.' The white structure of this American society, personified in every racist, must be at least part of what the New Testament meant by the demonic forces."[77]

For more than fifty years, Cone was the driving force behind Union Theological Seminary in New York City and the broader progressive Christian movement around the country. Feminist theology also emerged during this period in the 1960s and

'70s. Progressive Christian women began challenging the male-dominated arena of theology and Biblical studies in new ways.

Yet as the experiences of black women were not present in either black liberation theology or feminist theology, this gave rise to womanist theology. *Mujerista* theology did the same thing for Latina women, and queer liberation theology centered the experiences of LGBTQ people in theology. As more and more people pried the door to the theological academy open, Christian theology evolved and incorporated the richness of people who are followers of Jesus.

These liberationist theologies also intersected in diverse movements and people. Rev. Pauli Murray, for example, was a black, queer, feminist Episcopal priest who was active in the civil rights activist movement. Murray coined the term "Jane Crow" to drive home how Jim Crow laws impacted black women. Murray was first a lawyer, and then in 1977 was the first black woman to be ordained as an Episcopal priest, the year the first group of women were ordained in the Episcopal Church. In 2012 she was made a saint of the Episcopal Church with her feast day to be celebrated on July 1 each year.[78]

Rev. Murray is also one of the most influential progressive Christians erased from our public imagination. "Murray's open

> As more and more people pried the door to the theological academy open, Christian theology evolved and incorporated the richness of people who are followers of Jesus.

lesbian relationships and her gender nonconforming identity disrupted the dictates of respectability, making it easier to erase her five decades of important intellectual and political contributions from our broader narrative of civil rights," journalist Brittney Cooper writes.[79]

Cone, Gutiérrez, Murray, and many more Christians pushed the church forward as they addressed the sins of the past and present, shaping the future of the church. Cone captured the intersecting nature of these movements in an address to the United Methodist Church's "Love Your Neighbor" coalition in 2012, during the fight for LGBTQ rights in the church: "there can be no genuine understanding of Christian identity in America or the world and no deliverance from the brutal legacy of slavery and white supremacy and homophobia. . . . I say as long as you are silent and do nothing about homophobia and white supremacy and all these other evils, you are just as guilty as those who hung blacks on trees and queer people on picket fences."[80]

Cone's powerful words will echo long after his death in 2019. They changed the course of Christian theology forever and yet at the same time were deeply rooted in the Bible. In many ways, Cone called Christians to return home to the God of liberation we read about in the Bible and to become followers of Jesus.

We read in the Bible how in the creation narrative, God calls humanity and all of creation "good." We read of God creating a covenant with Abraham, of Israel's deliverance at the Red Sea, all recounted in the Hebrew Bible. Then, in the New Testament, we proclaim that death could not separate us from the love of

Christ embodied in the story of the resurrection. This is the telling of liberation in the Bible, and reading it makes it impossible to ignore how injustice in the world today screams out for God's liberating justice.

In today's public discourse, we hear about a distinction between the Black Lives Matter movement and a conservative reaction claiming that "All Lives Matter." What liberation theology teaches us is that the Bible is clear that because God loves all people, God sides with the oppressed in favor of their liberation. Sadly, many of the white, cishet (that is, cisgender and heterosexual), male theologians who dominate the theological academy have written off liberation theology as "contextual" theologies that arise from and are limited to various minority communities. White, cishet, male theology has no "context" in this framing. This, of course, couldn't be any farther from the truth. Liberation theology necessarily makes those who hold privilege uncomfortable, but God is in that discomfort. God is troubling the waters of the rich, of the United States, of white people, of straight people, of cisgender people, to cause a holy awakening of justice. And in every fight for "identity politics" today, we see the long tradition of people of faith demanding justice.

PART TWO

RECLAIMING OUR TRADITION

The bold tradition of progressive Christianity has been erased from our public imagination. The progressive movement has been cleansed of any religious motivations and the so-called secular left is pitted against the religious right. No, this book isn't a eulogy for the tradition we've lost, but a plan for how we reclaim it. Reclaiming our tradition requires believing the status quo can be changed. We can contest the meaning of "Christian" in the public square if progressive Christians in the United States come together and do what's necessary.

While I've been thinking about the state of progressive Christianity much of my life, the extent to which we've lost our tradition was made plain for me at one particular moment on October 4, 2018. The setting was the headquarters of the United Church of Christ in Cleveland, Ohio. Waiting in the lobby of the building before my meeting, I watched as a person came into the building off the street and approached one of the staff members. He asked, "Is this a church?" The UCC national headquarters staff

85

member responded in a hushed tone, "Yes, but not *that* kind of a church."

We are followers of Jesus. And while we should approach our calling with humility, there is no call to cower under the Goliath of conservative Christianity. Just as David had his sling, we need to harness the tools at our disposal. Thank God we're not starting from scratch!

"Is this a church?" "Do you go to church?" "What are you doing on Sunday?" We've all felt the tendency to say, "I'm not *that* kind of Christian." The ubiquity of conservative Christians can make us feel lonely and powerless to change our cultural definitions. There's a good chance if you're reading this book that you feel being a part of the Jesus movement is important to you. It's important to me. And being willing to claim that publicly is our call and challenge.

One Gospel image fits the state of progressive Christianity right now: the disciples locking themselves in a room after the crucifixion. John 20 tells us that the disciples were locked inside the room because they feared the religious authorities. Their leader had just been executed in public alongside two common criminals, by the most powerful government the world had ever seen. He said he would return, but how could the disciples trust that?

The fearful and demoralized state of progressive Christianity is warranted. Many American Christians are wondering if Christianity will ever try to look like the love of Jesus. We can draw inspiration from the disciples, who had their hope restored in the Gospel stories by Jesus's appearance to them after the crucifixion.

All of Jesus's post-resurrection visits to the disciples are strange, like the Road to Emmaus story, where his own followers don't recognize him. But in this story, Jesus suddenly appears before his disciples, coming into a locked room and telling them, "Peace be with you. As the Father has sent me, so I send you" (John 20:21). Jesus breathes on them and says, "Receive the Holy Spirit. If you forgive anyone's sins, their sins are forgiven; if you do not forgive them, they are not forgiven" (John 20:22–23, paraphrase).

Yes, Jesus is telling us today, it's scary out there. But this movement is up to you! Yes, the religious and political leaders are conspiring against us because we are a threat to the empire. Yes, I was just murdered for this revolutionary work. Yes, you might suffer the same fate that I did. And yes, you still have to leave the room. This mission of the Reign of God coming to earth, of the first being last, of setting the captives free, and of calling out the hypocrisy of religious leaders is up to you now!

I'm sure the disciples were worried. And I'm sure Jesus reminded them of what he said during the Sermon on the Mount in Matthew 6:25: "Therefore I tell you, do not worry about your life, what you will eat or what you will drink, or about your body, what you will wear. Is not life more than food, and the body more than clothing?" And in verses 33 and 34, "But strive first for the kingdom of God and his righteousness, and all these things will be given to you as well. So do not worry about tomorrow, for tomorrow will bring worries of its own. Today's trouble is enough for today."

We know Jesus reassured the disciples enough that they eventually left the room. They left the room and continued the movement that Jesus started. Jesus sent them, and they went. We've seen how, in just the last hundred years of this movement for love and inclusion, Jesus has sent so many people before us. And now, it's up to all of us.

It's time to leave the room. We can't tolerate the mission of Jesus in our country today being associated with the forces of exclusion and bigotry. We are called to leave behind our fear at how the religious leaders and empire are conspiring and follow Jesus. We are called to resist the hijacking of Jesus's message by conservatives and help reveal the radical nature of Jesus's ministry and a just faith. The following chapters are about how we can do just that.

CHAPTER 8

CONSISTENTLY PROGRESSIVE CHRISTIANS—IN LARGE NUMBERS

Loneliness plagues many progressive Christians. We feel like we're the only ones who are trying to follow Jesus's commandment to love and serve others in a sea of conservative Christians. There is good news on that front. And if there's one thing you take away from this book, let it be this: We exist. You are not alone. Millions of Americans identify as progressive Christians. In partnership with the Public Religion Research Institute (PRRI), I have exclusive new data that estimates how many consistently progressive Christians exist in the country, published and seen here for the first time. And . . . surprise!

Measuring the Number of Progressive Christians

There are actually more consistently progressive Christians than consistently conservative Christians in the United States.

Thanks to PRRI's data resources, my estimation is there are over thirty-five million American Christian adults age eighteen and above who are consistently progressive. There are strong contin-

gents of consistently progressive Christians across the different subsets of Christians (white mainline Protestants, black Protestants, Catholics, and white evangelical Protestants) that public opinion polling firms use to break down religious demographics.

> There are actually more consistently progressive Christians than consistently conservative Christians in the United States.

What does "consistently progressive" mean? Well, it can mean something different to everyone reading this book. Can you be progressive and support American military intervention abroad or any form of public support for private K–12 education in the United States? It can be helpful for us to debate such thorny questions, but my goal with this data is rather to offer a rough approximation of the number of consistently progressive Christian adults.

One method could be using "Democrat" as a proxy for "progressive." But that doesn't quite get at a fuller distinction because there are moderate Democrats. And, more importantly, there's a widespread misconception that while some portion of Christians in the United States vote for Democratic candidates for various reasons, they are conflicted about the progressive social views of the party, suggesting that "Democrat" may not be a helpful stand-in for "progressive."

Another approach is looking at political ideology and worship attendance. One recent study broke down the share of American adults using this approach and found that 6% of American adults self-identify as liberal or very liberal and self-report that they attend religious services several times a month or more often. There are shortcomings to this approach as well. There are progressive people of faith who value their religious tradition but don't attend services regularly for a variety of reasons. Six percent of the adult population is small, but still represents more than millions of Americans across all across the country.[81]

Estimating the size of a political and social constituency takes a different kind of test, so I set out to develop one for this book. Alongside the faith element, this test combines three issues to determine "progressive" status: women's reproductive health care, same-sex marriage, and immigration. This doesn't imply that these three issues are more important politically or morally than others but that abortion and same-sex marriage are issues around which conservative Christians draw their sharp lines. And one other factor has become increasingly determinative of a progressive direction in our political climate: the issue of immigration. It has been the defining issue of Trumpism and consistently cited as one of the most important issues to progressive Christians.

The survey resulted in an intentional approximation of the number of consistently progressive Christians in the United States. Here are several characteristics I believe we all share:

- Thirty-five million American adults who have practically no voice in the mainstream media.
- Thirty-five million American adults who hear public discussion of Christianity and don't want anything to do with what's being described.
- Thirty-five million American adults who are ready for change.
- And thirty-five million American adults who likely don't know there are thirty-five million American adults who share similar religious and political beliefs.

The Public Religion Research Institute provided the following chart based on a survey they conducted in 2018. PRRI polled a random sample of 2,020 adults eighteen years of age or older living in the United States. Among other questions, respondents were asked:

- Do you strongly favor, favor, oppose, or strongly oppose allowing gay and lesbian couples to marry?
- Do you think abortion should be legal in all cases, legal in most cases, illegal in most cases, or illegal in all cases?
- Do you strongly favor, favor, oppose, or strongly oppose allowing immigrants brought illegally to the US as children to gain legal-resident status?

In the exclusive analysis provided here, "consistently liberal" is defined as someone who favors or strongly favors same-sex marriage, says immigrants brought illegally to the US as children should be able to gain legal-resident status, and reports that abortion should be legal in all or most cases.

Percent of Americans Who Are Consistently Liberal by Religious Affiliation			
	Percent Consistently Liberal*	Percent of Population	N=
All Americans	32	100	2,020
All Religiously Affiliated	26	74	1,541
White Evangelical Protestant	9	17	364
White Mainline Protestant	31	13	311
Black Protestant	34	8	145
Catholic	30	19	422
*Non-Christian Religious***	33	13	221
Unaffiliated	51	24	433
Source: PRRI March 2018 Survey.			
* "Consistently liberal" is defined as someone who favors or strongly favors same-sex marriage, says immigrants brought illegally to the US as children should be able to gain legal status, and reports that abortion should be legal in all or most cases. ** Includes Jews, Muslims, Buddhists, Hindus, Unitarians, and adherents of other non-Christian religious traditions.			

There were more than 253.79 million adults age eighteen or over living in the US as of 2018 when this survey was conducted.[82] Based on this poll's findings, we can estimate there are more than thirty-five million consistently progressive (the term I prefer to PRRI's "consistently liberal") Christians in the United States. That's the cumulative total of 3.88 million white evangelicals, 10.22 million white mainline Protestants, 6.9 million black Protestants, and 14.46 million Catholics.

Since the time I first received an earlier version of the PRRI report three years ago, I've been telling people about it and there has been a uniform sense of bewilderment. "I wish some of them would speak up," a friend told me recently. Her surprise at these results was rooted in never having heard about this significant share of the population.

Yes, we need to speak up. But first we need to address this persistent feeling that consistently progressive Christians are anomalies. The popular narrative in our culture tells us that while some Democrats are Christians, they are conservative on "social issues" (a misnomer, of course, because all issues are social justice issues) like abortion and same-sex marriage; they're conflicted Christians. But the PRRI data highlights just how many consistently progressive Christians exist in complete defiance of the reigning cultural myths around religion, social justice issues, and politics.

Fosdick's question, "Shall the fundamentalists win?" is beginning to be answered: No. We've persisted in our faith and progressive values in spite of being told by conservative Christians that we're not "real Christians." It's a testament to the faith of progressive Christians that we have stayed true to the good news and following Jesus in the midst of such pressure. I hope that knowing there are millions upon millions of fellow Americans like you brings you a sense of greater belonging. I know this knowledge has brought me solace.

One major obstacle we face to movement building and belonging is that we are spread across Protestant denominations, non-denominational churches, and the Catholic Church. Many of us are in denominations where the official policy mirrors our beliefs, but others of us in "unfriendly" denominations continue to work within our official structures for greater inclusion and the common good. Examples are the work of Catholics for Choice and the many efforts on behalf of LGBTQ inclusion in non-affirming churches.

I've met many consistently progressive white evangelicals who are perhaps the most dismayed about their own tradition being associated with conservativism. While they are the least likely of the different types of Christians to pass this polling test by PRRI, I believe it's safe to assume that three million people is far more than one

> One major obstacle we face to movement building and belonging is that we are spread across Protestant denominations, non-denominational churches, and the Catholic Church. Many of us are in denominations where the official policy mirrors our beliefs, but others of us in "unfriendly" denominations continue to work within our official structures for greater inclusion and the common good.

might expect. I hope they can find common cause with the tens of millions of other Christians who have similar political views.

To advance the cause of progressive, social justice–oriented Christianity in public, we need new ways of connecting across our denominational silos and of seeing ourselves as part of the larger whole. The Episcopal Church's presiding bishop, the Most Reverend Michael Curry, describes his denomination this way: "As the Episcopal branch of the Jesus Movement, and followers of Jesus' Way, we seek to live like him. We're serious about moving out to grow loving, liberating, life-giving relationships with God (evangelism); to grow those relationships with each other (reconciliation); and to grow those relationships with all of creation (creation care)."[83]

We all recognize that the Jesus movement is wider than any of our denominations. I myself have moved from the United Methodist Church to a church that is dually aligned as United Church of Christ/Reformed Church of America to a church that is dually aligned with the Cooperative Baptist Fellowship and Alliance of Baptists. I've never felt like I've moved outside the stream of progressive Christianity, just within different branches of the Jesus movement.

There is a limit to how much an individual denomination can do in terms of representing progressive Christianity because, first, the official church advocacy and public engagement arms are inherently pulled to the middle of their own denominational equilibriums. And, second, the official denominational structures speak on behalf of their own members.

The power of conservative Christianity comes from building an overarching public narrative around their agenda that unites Christians of many individual churches and denominations. Progressive Christians need the kind of institutions that build and bind together a progressive Christian consciousness across our different denominations and our work with progressive Muslims, Jews, Sikhs, Buddhists, Unitarian Universalists, and other religious people to foster a great sense of being the religious people within the larger progressive movement in the United States.

There are two possible critiques of this data that I want to proactively address. The first shrugs off the numbers as unsurprising, responding that the numbers are bulked up by "cultural Christians"—a classic conservative Christian talking point echoed by the media. It consistently narrows a definition of "Christian" to mean conservative Christians. "Cultural Christian" has been a derogatory term for those giving in to "the secular culture" of liberalism; it seeks to erase the long history of progressive Christians actively pushing our faith and society into the modern world.

That might come from conservative Christians, but for media to echo the claim is irresponsible. Progressive Christians—in their full number—have just as much a right to be represented as conservatives, and any label that undermines the value of that Christian character should be avoided. It should be unacceptable to demean progressive Christians by insinuating a lack of genuineness, or diminishing the number by making a claim that we're not "real" Christians.

And, yes, not all thirty-five million consistently progressive Christians are going to engage in politics and public life *as* Christians. They might prefer to keep their faith private or not have a high level of investment in their faith. But if just one in ten of us really cared and was willing to get mobilized to have a greater impact on politics because of our faith, we would be part of a massive movement of people. The impact would shift the tectonic plates of Christianity and public life, carrying on the long tradition of faith and activism and civic engagement of Harry Emerson Fosdick, Martin Luther King, Pauli Murray, and others mentioned in Part One of this book.

Another possible reaction to the data is that most Christians in the United States are not *consistently* progressive or *consistently* conservative—they are somewhere in the middle. On one level, data might back up this point, but it doesn't address the wider data about the existence of progressive Christians. Importantly, our politics is largely determined not where the moderates stand on the issues—but where the poles are. The "Overton window" is the range of ideas tolerated in public discourse, and right now the Overton window concerning Christianity is moderate to far right. Increasing awareness that consistently progressive Christians exist will shift the entire equilibrium of how people see Christianity in public life to the left.

Measuring the Number of Conservative Christians

Progressive Christians are putting our faith into action just as conservative Christians are attempting to do the same. The second-most surprising data point from the PRRI poll was that consistently progressive Christian adults far outnumber consistently conservative Christian adults in the United States. PRRI used the same three questions from their 2018 poll and defined "consistently conservative" as someone who opposes or strongly opposes same-sex marriage, opposes or strongly opposes allowing immigrants brought illegally to the US as children to be able to gain legal-resident status, and reports that abortion should be illegal in all or most cases.

Percent of Americans Who Are Consistently Conservative by Religious Affiliation			
	Percent Consistently Conservative*	Percent of Population	N=
All Americans	10	100	2,020
All Religiously Affiliated	12	74	1,541
White Evangelical Protestant	25	17	364
White Mainline Protestant	10	13	311
Black Protestant	5	8	145

Catholic	7	19	422
Non-Christian Religious**	7	13	221
Unaffiliated	4	24	433

Source: PRRI March 2018 Survey.

* "Consistently conservative" is defined as someone who opposes or strongly opposes same-sex marriage, opposes or strongly opposes allowing immigrants brought illegally to the US as children to be able to gain legal-resident status, and reports that abortion should be illegal in all or most cases.

** Includes Jews, Muslims, Buddhists, Hindus, Unitarians, and adherents of other non-Christian religious traditions.

There are roughly eighteen million consistently conservative Christian adults in the United States. Here's the breakdown: 10.75 million white evangelicals, 3.29 million mainline Protestants, 1 million black Protestants, and 3.36 million Catholics. That's slightly more than half the size of the consistently progressive Christian adult population in the country. Again, there are many Christians who hold a mix of conservative and progressive beliefs. There are also many more issues that I could have included in the analysis. Setting those two important concerns aside, the results of this analysis reveal a Christian community in the United States that looks very different from the current state of our public imagination.

Now imagine how different our public imagination of Christianity in the United States would be if the thirty-five million consistently progressive Christians were as organized and vocal as the eighteen million. Rather than letting them wipe the floor with us, we need to know that our numbers almost double theirs. We've got to change, and that change starts with acknowledging we have the numbers on our side.

The problem is that the sides are not equally organized and vocal about their faith. Conservative Christians are loudly making claims about what it means to follow Jesus in our world today and exerting a far greater influence than are progressive Christians on what our cultural definition of "Christian" is. Conservative Christians have more organizations and media outlets and greater will to work together across denominational lines to advance their causes. In short, they have been better at influencing public opinion. That's where we turn next.

CHAPTER 9

HOW CONSERVATIVE CHRISTIANS HIJACKED OUR FAITH

*Beware of false prophets, who come to you in sheep's cloth-
ing but inwardly are ravenous wolves. You will know them
by their fruits. Are grapes gathered from thorns, or figs from
thistles? In the same way, every good tree bears good fruit,
but the bad tree bears bad fruit. A good tree cannot bear
bad fruit, nor can a bad tree bear good fruit. Every tree
that does not bear good fruit is cut down and thrown into
the fire. Thus you will know them by their fruits.*

—Matthew 7:15–20

Contesting who is speaking in accordance with God's love
and justice is not new. We see in this passage from Matthew
that Jesus warned his disciples to watch out for false prophets.
Conservative Christians are among today's false prophets. How
do we know? Jesus says we will know the false prophets by their

fruit. We have seen the fruit of conservative Christian ascendency in our country: a sharp decline in people self-identifying as Christians, climate destruction as conservative Christians spearheaded the war on science, and the tarnishing of the term "Christian" to such an extent that people of goodwill and conscience want no association with it. But to effectively confront these false prophets, we have to understand how they've been so successful in selling their brand of toxic Christianity.

Conservative Christians largely lost the battle over modernism in both the Protestant and Catholic traditions, but they found success in retreating and taking a defensive posture. On the Protestant side, the National Council of Churches, a coalition of what we now call "mainline Protestantism," was the leading voice for Protestant Christianity in the United States for decades after the modernist-fundamentalist controversy. And the mainline was truly "main" and encompassed a broad swath of moderate and progressive Protestants. Many progressives within these denominations were active in the bold traditions of the civil rights, peace, feminist, sanctuary, LGBTQ rights, and other social movements—but the mainline also included the more moderate elements of Protestantism. The Catholic Church also modernized with the Second Vatican Council.

The fact that conservative Christians have triumphed over a contemporary generation is quite remarkable and a testament to organizational infrastructure, funding levels, and cunning strategies. How did this happen? Among the strategies were the rebranding of *evangelical*, which limited and shifted our understanding of American Protestants in a conservative direction. Then Evangelicals teamed up with conservative Catholics, making criminalizing abortion and LGBTQ rights a litmus test for their unified Christian movement.

The "Evangelical" Rebrand

By the mid-twentieth century, *fundamentalist* had a bad rap. "Fundamentalists" were considered backwards and looked down upon in American culture. But the people behind fundamentalism did not fade quietly into oblivion. No, they still wanted to advance their cause against modern science and progressive values. So the worldlier, less antagonistic fundamentalists led the charge to brand conservative Christians as "evangelicals."

The goal of building up "evangelicalism" has always been clear: carve out a Christian identity apart from the heretical "mainline" types. Evangelicals use a number of terms to differentiate themselves from mainline Protestants; among the most common are "orthodox," "Bible-believing," and "traditional." But the meaning is always the same: only evangelicals are "real" Christians. While there is no clear-cut definition of what it means to be "evangelical" as compared to the fundamentals pamphlet circulated in the 1920s, the closest equivalent is the Bebbington quadrilateral, devised in 1989, defining the tenets of evangelicalism.[84] These include:

■ Biblicism: a particular regard for the Bible

■ Crucicentrism: a focus on the atoning work of Christ on the cross

■ Conversionism: the belief that human beings need to be converted

■ Activism: the belief that the gospel needs to be expressed in effort

You could easily call those "fundamentals" since they compose essentially the same conservative boundary-policing type of Christianity as their forebears, the fundamentalists, put forth before them. While Jesus said, "Come and follow me," conservatives have been known, in effect, for adding, "and follow this set of rules." It is this view of evangelicalism that has permeated our public consciousness to the point that it's not actively contested.

The great success of evangelicalism was getting broad buy-in across a range of theologically disparate groups such as Southern Baptists, Pentecostals, non-denominational prosperity gospel types, and many others to accept this "evangelical" branding. While evangelicalism is largely a refreshed fundamentalism, there are a few major differences in its approach: It's less overt in its statement of beliefs, and it appropriates popular culture to attract people into its churches. Evangelicals have excelled in marketing themselves. They rebranded when "fundamentalist" hindered their mission, and now actively downplay the anti-science, anti-LGBTQ, anti-women aspects of the movement.

The megachurch movement found great success in evangelicalism. One example is Hillsong Church, alternatively labeled "skinny jeans fundamentalism." This Pentecostal church started in a suburb of Sydney, Australia, and has spread rapidly around the world. The church is famous for its rock band music played in evangelical churches of every stripe. In the United States, it counts many celebrities, such as Justin Bieber, as members and focuses on "community" and inspirational sermons.

Hillsong is just one of many conservative churches that actively hide their theological convictions that are increasingly unpopular with young people with friendly exteriors, coffee shops, tattooed pastors, and other welcoming "come as you are" vibes. A number of my friends have confessed being tricked by these churches and not realizing how conservative their theology turned out to be. From their precursors located in suburban, white centers where conservative churches flourished, these churches are now entering urban centers with a hipster-facade conservative Christianity.

The hidden agendas include an unarticulated (but real) hatred of LGBTQ people, the quiet refusal of many of them to allow women to preach, and the lack of acknowledgment of their conservative denominational backers.

Regrettably, the Word *Evangelical* Has Been Tarnished

This hijacking of the word *evangelical* is a cause of lament for progressive Christians. The word comes from the Greek word *euangelion*, meaning "good news." It was a term used by Catholics, Protestants, and other Christians of all varieties to mean spreading the message of Jesus. For conservative Christians, this understanding of "good news" was related to a ticket out of hell, purchased by believing the "right" things about history, God, and Jesus. For conservative Christians this meant that only people who believed the "correct" things would go to heaven and escape hell.

Progressive Christians understood the good news as the truths Jesus preached: liberation to the oppressed, setting the captives free, and the total reorientation of society from favoring the rich to favoring the poor. So you might say all Christians are evangelical; it's just different "good news" the two groups are evangelizing.

Of course, the "good news" meaning of *evangelical* that existed before the fundamentalist takeover of the label is still used today. Most notably, the mainline Protestant Lutheran denomination is the Evangelical Lutheran Church in America. Some notable leaders in the mainline denominations like Rev. Dr. William Barber II, who is ordained in the Disciples of Christ denomination, use the term to mean, literally, the good news of the gospel of Jesus. This leads some people to differentiate capital E "Evangelical" (the Conservative Christian political movement) from "evangelical," in order to keep the term close to its original meaning.

Many in the mainline traditions love the term *evangelical*, with its original meaning, and self-identify with the term—despite its association with Liberty University, Jerry Falwell Jr., and the Southern Baptist Convention. Yet, in many ways the term has now become irredeemable. The fundamentalists-turned-evangelicals have been so successful in advancing their own understanding of the word that it's impossible to gain airtime to contest its new meaning. And as progressives have so much work to do to reclaim the word "Christian" or even the phrase "follower of Jesus," we should be honest in admitting that as a term, *evangelical* today is the rebranded version of fundamentalism rooted in white supremacy.

Inside the World of the Evangelical Elite

This conclusion wasn't easy for me to come to personally. It came after several years of seeing from inside the highest rungs of American Evangelicalism that it is the major cause of our distorted view of Christianity in the United States. I spent three years as an invited guest inside this space through my work at the National Immigration Forum in Washington, DC. The Forum brings together a diverse range of constituencies to advocate for comprehensive immigration reform and a pathway to citizenship for undocumented immigrants.

Like President George W. Bush did, a number of high-profile conservative Christian organizations embraced the cause of comprehensive immigration reform in the mid- to late-2000s. The Forum organized conservative Christians in support of immigrant rights, and I remain proud of the work I accomplished there. Political commentators have credited this conservative Christian support of comprehensive immigration reform with helping it gain broad, bipartisan traction in the Senate in 2013. I worked with an amazing team of Christians of all types, as well as non-Christians, behind the scenes to mobilize conservative Catholic and evangelical support for the bill. While I left the Forum to go to seminary one month before Trump announced his campaign for the presidency by calling Mexicans "rapists," the Forum's work to mobilize conservative Christians continues.

What I discovered working with groups like the National Association of Evangelicals, the Ethics and Religious Liberty Commission of the Southern Baptist Convention, World Vision, and many individual "thought leaders" was their active discounting of progressive Christians. Many progressive Christian groups had been active in the immigrant rights battle for decades, but this tradition was ignored by conservative Christians. I saw firsthand how evangelicals viewed non-evangelical Protestants as not Christians. And I saw conservative Catholic leaders ignore the work of progressive Catholics by shutting them out of meetings.

While rarely stated explicitly, the agenda to create this narrative had wide ramifications. They praise "Christian" X, Y, or Z phenomena or certain "Christian" figures in our public life, yet omit those who don't fit their conservative Christian definition. "Christian" is aggressively pushed in our culture as synonymous with evangelicalism. "Christian music" references worship singers and fundamentalist recording artists, not Beyoncé, Taylor Swift, or Broadway star Kristin Chenoweth, all of whom are Christian musicians. "Christian colleges" doesn't reference mainline Protestant-founded colleges across the country, like my alma mater American University, which is affiliated with the

United Methodist church and is devoted to liberalism and pluralism. "Christian colleges" are evangelical schools that, among other checklist items, don't want to allow LGBTQ student groups to meet. "Christian politicians" aren't Barack Obama, Nancy Pelosi, or Elizabeth Warren. Rather, "Christian politicians" are conservatives like Marco Rubio and Mike Pence. As those of us who are progressive Christians have no problem calling conservative Christians "Christians", this only reinforces the asymmetry of our public discourse around Christianity.

Whether coming from your progressive friends, the media, or any other source, just try to imagine counting all the times you hear "Christian" associated with a conservative cause, politician, or movement vs. the times you hear "Christian" in relation to progressive causes, politicians, or movements.

I also witnessed the extent to which conservative Christians accomplished this divide-and-conquer takeover by out-organizing progressives and moderates. They've successfully built organizations and media outlets to convey their message. Events like the National Prayer Breakfast and Values Voters Summit serve as annual reminders of the conservative Christian agenda. They also work behind the scenes through secretive outreach to politicians, and journalists use that to shape our public imagination. Their organizing strategy is also simple to understand. While I was working with conservative Christians to pass immigration reform, I saw how immigration never rose close to the level of their marquee issues.

Conservative Christians consistently pick anti-abortion and anti-LGBTQ rights as two litmus-test issues that are easily identifiable. All other issues are subordinated to these two causes. While it's a myth that the religious right came about because of abortion and LGBTQ rights (see chapter 3 on the civil rights movement), conservative Christians have made their public witness easy to digest. Organizing against things is also easier than trying to advance proactive causes. Conservative Christians can just focus on these over and over again and build a base of support around them. They've done such a good job that "evangelical" is now synonymous with conservative Christian in our public imagination.

The Westboro Baptist Church Effect

Conservative Christians have been so loud and have attracted so much media attention that they've distorted the coverage of Christianity at-large. The "Westboro Baptist Church Effect" is named after the virulently anti-LGBTQ group that is actually a small group in terms of membership but that has a huge presence. Westboro Baptist Church is not representative of conservative Christianity in terms of the extreme nature of their positions; they are on the far-right fringe. But they are the gold standard of how conservative Christians—even those with less extreme views on LGBTQ rights and other issues—capture media attention.

As with Westboro, much of the coverage of conservative Christianity is negative in the mainstream media. This leads to a perception among conservative Christians that the mainstream "secular" media hates religion. This then leads to more positive, nuanced coverage of conservative Christians to prove that mainstream media outlets aren't biased. The result is a sheer overwhelming imbalance of coverage in favor of conservative Christians over progressive Christians, and it impacts our cultural perception of Christianity at-large.

As a religion writer, I've tried to do my part in shifting this imbalance. I contributed a religion-angle perspective to the *Washington Post*'s coverage of the Alabama senate election in 2017, where Roy Moore, the far-right Alabama judge credibly accused of sexually assaulting three women when they were fourteen, sixteen, and twenty-eight respectively, was running for office. The religion and politics news beat heated up because Moore is an outspoken conservative Christian, and the media wanted to know whether evangelicals in Alabama would stick by him.

It turned out that Roy Moore's opponent, Doug Jones, was active in the Methodist church and deeply committed to following Jesus, without using "following Jesus" as a political or sensationalist weapon to stir up media attention.

My *Washington Post* story, "Roy Moore Isn't the Only Christian Running for Senate in Alabama," included interviews with his campaign spokesperson and fellow church members.[85]

"It's fair to say Doug has been a very active Christian . . . but . . . not in the sense of, 'You either believe the way I do or there's no room for you,'" his spokesman, Sebastian Kitchen, told me. "As a person of deep faith,

Doug believes in Christ's call to minister to all people—regardless of their background, race, or religion. Unfortunately, Roy Moore instead uses religion to divide people, instead of trying to join together to make progress."

After the story ran, a prominent religion reporter at a national news outlet emailed me, "I never even thought to ask about whether or where Jones went to church." Asking Democrats about their faith is rarely part of our public discourse because, again, we see religion as the province of the conservative movement.

We'd heard endlessly about the 81% of white evangelicals who voted for Donald Trump for president. That's what we hear from media, but that isn't the full story. A majority of "other Christians"—including non-white evangelical Christians and progressive Christians—voted for Hillary Clinton for president in 2016.

> Religion reporting to try to lift up the work progressive churches are doing is a drop in the bucket compared to the torrent of coverage we see about evangelicals and their power in American politics. And this focus distorts the public's understanding of American Christianity. What we need is systemic change in newsrooms across America.

I've long been frustrated by how media covers Christianity with a preference for evangelicals over mainline progressive Protestants like Doug Jones and Hillary Clinton, and rarely presses conservative Christians for the harm they've done, including contributing to anti-LGBTQ violence. Religion reporting to try to lift up the work progressive churches are doing is a drop in the bucket compared to the torrent of coverage we see about evangelicals and their power in American politics. And this focus distorts the public's understanding of American Christianity. What we need is systemic change in newsrooms across America.

And I'm not the only one who sees distorted coverage of American Christianity. America's most infamous media critic—Donald Trump—does too.

An in-depth report by CNN about Trump's own religious convictions started with a fascinating interaction. "Two days before his presidential inauguration, Donald Trump greeted a pair of visitors at his office in Trump Tower," the report began. "As a swarm of reporters waited in the gilded lobby, the Rev. Patrick O'Connor, the senior pastor at the First Presbyterian Church in Queens, and the Rev. Scott Black Johnston, the senior pastor of Manhattan's Fifth Avenue Presbyterian Church, arrived to pray with the next president."[86]

The reporter, MJ Lee, then set the scene: "From behind his desk on the 26th floor, Trump faced the Celtic cross at the top of the steeple of Johnston's church, located a block south on Fifth Avenue. When Johnston pointed it out to Trump, the President-elect responded by marveling at the thick glass on the windows of his office—bulletproof panels installed after the election. It was clear that Trump was still preoccupied with his November victory, and pleased with his performance with one constituency in particular."

"I did very, very well with evangelicals in the polls," Trump told the pastors, according to the CNN report. The pastors then "gently reminded Trump that neither of them was an evangelical." This led Trump to answer, "Well, what are you then?"

"They explained they were mainline Protestants, the same Christian tradition in which Trump, a self-described Presbyterian, was raised and claims membership," CNN reported. "Like many mainline pastors, they told the President-elect, they lead diverse congregations."[87]

Well, what are you then? That question has stuck with me in the years since I first read this CNN report. Trump, who devours hours and hours of cable news TV every day and is obsessed with *The New York Times,* had no awareness that non-evangelical Protestants exist. CNN attributed this to his lack of personal religious convictions: "Trump is unique among modern American presidents for his seeming lack of deep religious orientation."[88] Yet a look at CNN's coverage of religion and politics provides a mirror to the issue. The obsession with evangelicals on the part of the media has been a significant factor in Trump thinking two pastors in the Presbyterian Church (U.S.A.) denomination were evangelical, and resulted in his follow-up question, "What are you then?"

According to PRRI, white evangelical Protestants make up 17% of the US population, and white mainline Protestants make up 13%, with non-white Protestants making up 15%.[89] From a numbers perspective, and a media-fairness perspective there's no way to justify the disproportionate coverage of white evangelicals, however easy it is to understand the Westboro Baptist Church Effect.

Westboro Baptist Church has likely generated more media coverage than any small church in America over the past three decades. That's a startling accomplishment for advancing their message, given the fact that the church doesn't have many members beyond one family. As progressive Christians with disproportionately low coverage, we need to reflect on how Westboro punches above its weight class. As a gay man, I understand that Westboro's hate is the reality that has helped define what it means to be a Christian in the public square.

The first contributing factor of the Westboro Baptist Church Effect is that they are easy to understand. Mass media does not lend itself to nuance. Westboro Baptist Church makes it clear they hate gay people and believe God is punishing America for accepting LGBTQ people. There's no doubt where they stand or what their mission statement is. Any general-assignment reporter can cover one of their protests without much religious literacy training. They fit the dominant narrative of what it means to be Christian in America today.

Within the homogeneity of conservative Christians (however extreme their hatred), they are clear and consistent around their key issues, abortion and LGBTQ rights, which make it easy for reporters and news commentators to focus. This was manufactured to increase cohesion and decrease tension, but it presents easily digestible nuggets for the news media.

The diversity of progressive Christianity—not to mention being one piece of the larger religious left and the ever-larger progressive movement in America—makes it difficult for the press to cover.

One day people are protesting about the environment, another day it's a Black Lives Matter protest, and finally it's a protest for passing universal health care.

Second, the Westboro Baptist Church Effect intentionally causes conflict wherever church members go. Every good news story has at least two characters: a protagonist and an antagonist. Westboro picks provocative battles and creates a standoff with counter-protestors. Conservative Christians have, in general, been excellent at consistently naming the enemy in our midst: secular liberals who want to destroy religion and America in the process. Everything from Starbucks holiday cups to rallying around Trump in the midst of his "locker room talk" is a part of a cosmic battle.

> The diversity of progressive Christianity—not to mention being one piece of the larger religious left and the ever-larger progressive movement in America—makes it difficult for the press to cover. One day people are protesting about the environment, another day it's a Black Lives Matter protest, and finally it's a protest for passing universal health care.

Progressive Christians once understood they were also in a cosmic battle with both fundamentalists and an unjust society that favored the rich and powerful. We named names and picked fights. Under Trump we've seen a return to drawing battle lines. Progressive Christians have mobilized and caused conflict, bringing a slight uptick to progressives of faith in news coverage since Trump's election.

The Westboro Baptist Church Effect also works because they show up when it matters in an opportunistic way. Picketing at Matthew Shepard's funeral was a despicable yet bold choice. Westboro shows up at national events and inserts themselves into the conversation with a unique angle as Christians. This is one reason why Christians protesting at the border receive increased media attention. The story is a big media story already, and reporters are always looking for interesting angles for ongoing stories.

And the Westboro Baptist Church Effect is not just a media strategy. If progressives ask, "How do we get more media coverage?" they are asking the wrong question. The question should always be, "How do we conduct public activities and prophetic actions that will then generate positive media coverage for the issues and campaigns we feel need to get more attention?" Westboro Baptist Church doesn't just send out press releases; they have legal and organizing activities that undergird all of their appearances in the media. They show up at funerals to claim God murdered fallen soldiers as punishment for the military accepting LGBTQ people. In the organizing world, we'd call that a direct-action field strategy. And it's backed up by a tough legal strategy that made it all the way to the Supreme Court.

Their case reached the Supreme Court in 2010. At the time, I was attending college in Washington, DC. My professor, Susan Benesch, director of the Dangerous Speech Project, offered to camp outside the Supreme Court with a few students in sleeping bags so that we could get in to witness the historic free-speech case. In the morning, the Phelps family arrived, and I watched as the media circus descended on them. They were the center of attention, and I realized that no matter how the case turned out, they had achieved their goal of getting the message out.

Every day conservative Christians are the people setting themselves on fire in the town square. It's impossible to look away. And while some of them are doing it solely for the attention and fame, I believe many of them care deeply about the issues that motivate them, such as controlling women's bodies and rolling back LGBTQ rights. Many sincerely fear a pluralistic society where Christians are just one of many religious groups, and a social norm that accepts people who do not attend any religious services. This deep indoctrination that the "secular" culture is destroying America motivates them to go to extremes to get attention and raise awareness of their cause.

Ridicule it or cry about it, it's ultimately more important to learn from our response to the Westboro Baptist Church Effect. While progressives aren't looking for an equivalent to their "God Hates Fags" slogan, they might look to something that is easily understood by media and generates long-term coverage. Of course, I'm not calling for us to answer hate with hate, but we have to figure out how to drown out the hate and make our voices heard alongside the conservative Christian voices. To accomplish that goal, progressive Christians need to better understand what values capture the media's attention. The election of Donald

Trump has presented an opportunity for progressive Christians to reclaim our space in the media.

The Turning of the Tide for Conservative Christians: Trumpism

The election of Donald Trump in 2016 was the natural culmination of conservative Christianity's trajectory over the past hundred years. Conservative Christianity is a theological and political movement that actively and consistently rebels against science as incompatible with the Bible's account of creation and against the Social Gospel as some kind of distraction from saving souls. None of the branding or emotional worship experiences in evangelical churches will cover that up.

Trump's appeal to conservative Christians is a nostalgic appeal to a less diverse and more "Christian" America—and by "Christian" they certainly mean Christian Evangelicals. The thinly veiled white supremacy that has accompanied conservative Christians has always been chaplain to this form of empire—especially when coupled with Trump's telling the first Muslim congresswomen and the two other members of the "The Squad" to "go back" to their countries of origin (never mind that three of the four were born in the United States). Promoting Christian nationalism and the Muslim ban are two sides of the same coin.

In August 2019, Trump retweeted a conspiracy theorist supporter of his calling him the "King of Israel" and "the second coming of God," and called himself the "the chosen one."[90]

Authoritarian tendencies fit perfectly in a tradition that has always been top-down and patriarchal, where white men control the ground rules of what it means to be Christian. In a religious culture where adoration of the strict father is seen as the only acceptable posture, the rules he sets are never to be broken. This ties into the ways conservative Christians are obsessed with doctrinal purity and maintaining patriarchal gender roles.

Some wonder how a person credibly accused of sexual misconduct by twenty-four women could have been the natural choice for conservative Christians.

Trump's conservative Christian backers looked past his infamous words on the *Access Hollywood* tape, "You know, I'm automatically attracted to beautiful—I just start kissing them. It's like a magnet. Just kiss. I don't even wait. And when you're a star, they let you do it. You can do anything. Grab 'em by the pussy. You can do anything."[91] And Trump has rewarded them, by nominating conservative judges and taking a hard-line stance on abortion politics. In August 2018, Trump brought one hundred evangelical leaders to the White House for a state-like dinner. Conservative Christians have cemented themselves as the most important constituency in the conservative movement in America, ahead of gun-rights activists, small-government libertarians, and other interest groups.

This culmination is also a moment of opening for progressive Christians. The religious right has hitched their fortunes to the Trump train and there's no turning back. But to contest the dominant form of Christianity in the public square and its toxic alliance with Trump, we're going to have to use words.

CHAPTER 10

WHAT IT MEANS TO RAISE YOUR VOICE

Set aside whatever you feel about Hillary Clinton, the political candidate. I'd like you to instead consider Hillary Clinton, the Christian. She's a lifelong, active member of the United Methodist Church. Throughout her long career she has discussed how her faith impacts her public service and political views.

"I have always had a deep personal faith that was rooted in the Methodist church in large measure because I was christened into it, I grew up in it," Clinton told *The New York Times* in 2007. "You know, if you look at the Methodist book of discipline it talks about the four contributing streams of faith—scripture, tradition, experience and reason. I always resonated to the fact that it was both revelatory and scripture-based but that you were invited to use your power of reason to think through your faith and to work through what it meant to you and how you would live it in your daily life."[92]

Clinton often describes her political awakening happening when her social justice–oriented youth pastor took her to see the Rev. Dr. Martin Luther King Jr. speak in Chicago in 1962. "Until then, I had been dimly aware of the social revolution occurring in our country, but Dr. King's words illuminated the struggle taking place and challenged our indifference," Clinton wrote in her memoir, *Living History*.[93] After the 2016 campaign ended, Clinton disclosed that she might have pursued a career as a minister if it weren't for going into politics.[94]

The Republican Party's candidate for president in 2016 was Donald J. Trump. He's a thrice-married man who brags about sexually assaulting women, craves money and attention, refuses to apologize for egregious bias and unethical behavior, said he could get away with shooting someone on Fifth Avenue in New York City, and mocked the piety of his running mate, Mike Pence. I believe all of his opponents and even many of his supporters would agree that he was the most irreligious and immoral candidate for president in modern American history.

This should have been a giant opening for Clinton and the Democratic Party to reshape how Americans see the intersection of Christianity and politics. Clinton had prepared her entire life to make the case for why her faith informed her campaign and why many Americans' religious values were on the line. She couldn't have faced an opponent more unlikely to win religious people over. And yet, somehow, Hillary Clinton's defeat by Donald Trump was heralded as a victory for American

Christians. Her faith took a backseat during the campaign to Trump's embrace of the religious right and its alliance with the Republican Party.

Ten months and, in Clinton's own words, many glasses of Chardonnay later, Clinton processed her surprise defeat by Trump at the Riverside Church in New York City. In conversation with Rev. Ginger Gaines-Cirelli, the senior pastor of Foundry United Methodist Church, Clinton displayed the kind of intelligent discussion of faith that makes her such a contrast to Trump.

"There is a large group of people with a very strong opinion that if you're a Christian, if you profess your faith, you can only have one set of political beliefs, and if you deviate from those political beliefs you are somehow not really a Christian," Clinton said at Riverside.[95] Clinton didn't mean her own political beliefs. She lamented the way Donald Trump dominated the "Christian vote" debate throughout the election. In other words, "conservative Christian" was synonymous with "Christian" in most people's eyes.

"I reject that completely," Clinton added. But during the same conversation she also offered somewhat of an explanation of why she lost the faith debate to the least likely of men. "I was raised to believe that actions spoke louder than words," she said. "If you were a person of faith, that should be evident in how you treated other people and what kind of life you lived. So, I didn't go around talking about it a lot, but it certainly was foremost in my mind. I've tried to express it, sometimes more effectively than other times, over the course of the last twenty or thirty years. But I've tried to be guided by it, even more importantly."

Progressive Christians seek to live out this sentiment by supporting social justice movements and continuing to be the body of Christ. We love to be doers. "But be doers of the word, and not merely hearers." Taken from the book of James 1:22, this is a favorite verse for many progressive Christians.

Preaching this gospel of radical inclusion, an equitable economy, setting the oppressed free, and tearing down every border and boundary that separates us requires a lot of *doing*. But it also requires a raised voice. There are protests to plan, worship services to hold, and people to visit in the hospital and in prison. And please, please, please don't get me wrong. *Talking* without actually *doing* is the worst option possible. We need to live out being the Beloved Community, and that means getting our own faith communities in order before we try to engage the public. Jesus has harsh words for hypocrites and religious leaders who don't practice what they preach.

> Preaching this gospel of radical inclusion, an equitable economy, setting the oppressed free, and tearing down every border and boundary that separates us requires a lot of *doing*. But it also requires a raised voice.

We desperately need to do both.

This is the point where I let you know I do have an "ask" for you. Since you've made it this far in the book, you likely share some Christian conviction and a zeal for action, so my ask is that you use your voice, in whatever way you can, louder and more often than you have to this point.

We need to use words. Christianity isn't going to get untangled from conservativism without us proactively litigating the case in the public square. We need to be thinkers and pray-ers and doers and word users. We are called not just to act for social justice, but to contest the hijacking of Christianity.

The Hebrew prophets didn't just let their actions speak for themselves. In Isaiah 10 we see some of the strongest words used to talk about society:

Ah, you who make iniquitous decrees,
    who write oppressive statutes,
to turn aside the needy from justice
    and to rob the poor of my people of their right,
that widows may be your spoil,
    and that you may make the orphans your prey!
What will you do on the day of punishment,
    in the calamity that will come from far away?
To whom will you flee for help,
    and where will you leave your wealth,
so as not to crouch among the prisoners
    or fall among the slain?
For all this his anger has not turned away;
    his hand is stretched out still. (Isaiah 10:1–4)

In strong words, we condemn conservative Christian hypocrisy that betrays Jesus's words, and the political leaders who defy the common good. We have to use our words and use them as Christians. Use words to condemn the injustice of the world. Use words to bring a new world into being.

Jesus tells his disciples in John 13:34–35, "I give you a new commandment, that you love one another. Just as I have loved you, you also should love one another. By this everyone will know that you are my disciples, if you have love for one another." We know that love is the mark of a true Christian, that we will be seen as Jesus's disciples if we follow him in love. But love is an action word. When prominent progressives speak explicitly about their faith, it makes waves.

Popular progressive writer and cable news commentator Ana Marie Cox wrote an amazing essay for the *Daily Beast* about coming out as a Christian. "Here is why I believe I am a Christian: I believe I have a personal relationship with my Lord and Savior," she wrote. "I believe in the grace offered by the Resurrection. I believe that whatever spiritual rewards I may reap come directly from trying to live the example set by Christ. Whether or not I succeed in living up to that example is primarily between Him and me."[96]

Cox's essay stunned me because I rarely heard political commentators other than conservatives talk about the role of faith in their lives. I met many Christians working in politics in DC, but few like Cox who were willing to draw attention to their faith. "God does not see charming dissonance in being a liberal who follows Christ; He's not looking for that *New York Times* Style section trend story. I do not get to think of myself as 'edgy' for being just another believer. There is nothing to reconcile."[97]

Cox's essay was penned in 2015, and since then we've seen more people come out publicly in the wake of Trumpism. Pete Buttigieg's candidacy curiously elicited strong negative reaction from conservative Christians, as his Christianity represented a singular threat to their whole worldview—Pete is an out, gay, married convicted Christian who believes in following Jesus and talking about how his faith informs his political views.

"I think it's unfortunate that [the Democratic Party] has lost touch with a religious tradition that I think can help explain and relate our values," Buttigieg told *The Washington Post*. "At least in my interpretation, it helps to root [in religion] a lot of what it is we do believe in, when it comes to protecting the sick and the stranger and the poor, as well as skepticism of the wealthy and the powerful and the established."[98]

"The left is rightly committed to a separation of church and state," he told *USA TODAY*. "But we need to not be afraid to invoke arguments that are convincing on why Christian faith is going to point you in a progressive direction."[99] While it's important for progressive Christians in the public eye to represent our tradition and contest the stranglehold that conservative Christians have on our faith, all of us can do something.

Our mission requires actions, prayers, and yes, words. Our words are not the conviction that if you don't agree, you are going to hell—or that our religion is somehow better to the detriment of someone else—but they are a reflection of what drives us. We have to use words to talk about our faith. We don't have to be cable TV pundits to do this; we can do this in everyday interactions at our workplaces, on our college campuses, or with our families.

Use words when the topics of religion and politics come up in your social circle or workplace. The era of not talking about religion, politics, and sex in "polite" company is long over. Use words to confront an anti-LGBTQ "Christian" group on your campus and call them out for their hate in the name of Christ. Use words to meet with the editors at your local newspaper to ensure they are fairly covering the diversity of Christian belief in your community. Defend and advance progressive goals as consistent with Christian teaching—not because we believe in theocracy, but because our faith makes us progressive. When you show up at your local protest, put a Bible verse on the sign. Make it clear to the world you're engaging the public as a Christian.

> Use words when the topics of religion and politics come up in your social circle or workplace. The era of not talking about religion, politics, and sex in "polite" company is long over.

"Use words" is shorthand for letting people know that what you're doing and advocating for is done in the name of following Jesus. One way that churches have used words creatively is placing provocative progressive messages on their church marquees. Another is marching in Pride parades. It's one form of evangelism even the most progressive of us can get behind. At my Baptist church in Louisville, I can't tell you how many people have said a version of "I never knew a church like this existed." The only way we'll clue people in is by being vocal and public.

My personal attempt to "use words" has been through sharing how my own coming-out story relates to being a vocal progressive. I grew up in a denomination that told me a very important part of who I was—my sexual orientation—made me "incompatible with Christian teaching." I appreciate all the saints who went before and paved the road that I could walk down as an openly gay Christian. I know I feel the responsibility to be a voice for people wondering if their own LGBTQ identity and progressive political identity are consistent with following Jesus. I've shared this story in speeches and newspaper op-eds because I feel the responsibility to other LGBTQ Christians to use my voice.

As part of the LGBTQ community, many of us progressive Christians are narrative busters. We don't fit our American culture's binary of religious right and secular left, a narrative peddled by conservatives and swallowed whole by the media and pundit class. I believe we are called to share our stories—as we are each able to do in our own spheres of influence—and help change the definition of "Christian" in our culture.

CHAPTER 11

SKEPTICISM FROM OUR FELLOW PROGRESSIVE CHRISTIANS

Progressive Christians being more vocal about our faith in the public square will go a long way in challenging the dominance of the Christian right. As I've made this case for more vocal progressive Christian public engagement, I've encountered a number of important questions raised by fellow progressive Christians. In Scripture we see the proverb "Iron sharpens iron, and one person sharpens the wits of another" (Proverbs 27:17). We need to have these debates, and skepticism is warranted. The desire to let our "actions do the talking" is just one vein of skepticism. Progressive Christians who raise these concerns are well-intentioned and help us to refine our approach.

"Religion Doesn't Belong in Politics"

The separation of church and state is a critical aspect of the United States government. Article VI of the US Constitution provides that "no religious Test shall ever be required as a Qualification to any Office or public Trust under the United States," and the first amendment to the US Constitution states, "Congress shall make no law respecting an establishment of religion, or prohibiting the free exercise thereof."[100] The Constitution guarantees the right of religious people to practice our faith freely and without coercion from the government having a preference for one religion over another. This religious freedom extends to people who don't want to practice any religion. Progressive Christians rightly champion the rights of religious minorities and people of no faith when they are threatened by policies such as President Trump's Muslim ban.

Like with any good idea, some progressive Christians take the idea of the separation of church and state too far. They may be active in church and political life, but they somehow bifurcate these parts of their lives. Since all progressive Christians value the separation of church and state, it can be difficult to respond to this objection when it is applied to any faith-based appeal in the public square.

Beneath this concern is often a deep reluctance to mirror the approach of conservative Christians. For anyone who has had this conversation, you can appreciate the questions these people bring. They've seen how the religious right has made an idol out of politics and religious power. We can and we must learn lessons from the religious right, including the commitment to not sacrifice our values for political power. But the lesson we learn from conservative Christian social engagement is not to keep religion and politics apart, but that the issues driving conservative Christians seem in direct conflict with the teachings of Jesus.

We can't make these constitutional protections into an infinitely high wall that puts religion on one side and politics on the other. That kind of wall, like most walls, draws an artificial boundary that doesn't reflect how our values, politics, and faith work. Which side of the wall does "advancing the common good" or "defending human dignity" live on? Those are both essential to living out our faith as progressive Christians and have huge impacts on our political life together.

This doesn't argue for something being the law of the land because of a Christian's belief. For most progressive Christians who value pluralism, it's a very different claim from arguing how religion influences all part of people's values, actions, and participation in democracy. We can and should advocate for common-good policies. The values instilled in me through my church, through the study of Scripture, and through my ongoing attempt to follow Jesus, guide everything I do in life. The idea that I need to separate my religious values from my activism doesn't even make logical sense. My advocacy is explicitly as a Christian because I believe it is very much part of what Jesus means by sharing the good news.

"The church must be reminded that it is not the master or the servant of the state, but rather the conscience of the state," Rev. Dr. King preached. "It must be the guide and the critic of the state, and never its tool. If the church does not recapture its prophetic zeal, it will become an irrelevant social club without moral or spiritual authority."[101] King captures how the church should play an active role in the political sphere while remaining vigilant about becoming the governing political power at prayer.

Expressing our conscience and values as progressive Christians and explicitly as progressive Christians is important because it is the authentic expression of what drives our politics. Imagine if Rev. Dr. King had checked his religiosity at the entrance to the public square. The other, equally compelling reason to express our values is that, in addition to authenticity, progressive Christians have an obligation to stand up to the toxic form of Christian nationalism in our nation. If "Christian nationalism" is the only form of Christian expression in public life, then all Christians can easily become unwittingly associated with this dangerous cause.

Michelle Goldberg, a New York Times columnist, writes in her 2006 book, Kingdom Coming, that Christian nationalism "claims supernatural sanction for its campaign of national renewal and speaks rapturously about vanquishing the millions of Americans who would stand in its way."[102]

In an article for the Huffington Post that year, Goldberg writes, "At one rally at the statehouse in Austin, Texas, a banner pictured a fierce eagle perched upon a bloody cross. For a liberal, such imagery smacks of fascist agitprop. But plenty of deeply committed Christians also object to it as a form of blasphemy. It's important, I think, to separate their faith from the authoritarian impulses of the Christian nationalist movement. Christianity is a religion. Christian nationalism is a political program, and there is nothing sacred about it."[103]

Under Trump, the backers of Christian nationalism found an ally in the White House, helping push a far-right "Christian" agenda in state legislatures across the country through a series of bills called Project Blitz. "The idea behind Project Blitz is to overwhelm state legislatures with bills based on centrally manufactured legislation," Katherine Stewart wrote recently in *The New York Times*. "An Oklahoma measure, which has passed the legislature and is awaiting the governor's signature, allows adoption and foster care agencies to discriminate on the basis of their own religious beliefs. Others, such as a Minnesota bill that would allow public schools to post 'In God We Trust' signs on their walls, have provoked hostile debates in local and national media, which is in many cases the point of the exercise."[104]

Christian nationalism makes an idol of a twisted form of patriotism that turns following Christ into a tool of coercion. Thankfully, in mid-2019 a group of Christian organizations and leaders launched "Christians Against Christian Nationalism." Their organizing statement included this: "Whether we worship at a church, mosque, synagogue, or temple, America has no second-class faiths. All are equal under the US Constitution. As Christians, we must speak in one voice condemning Christian nationalism as a distortion of the gospel of Jesus and a threat to American democracy."[105]

There are many more examples we can draw upon, including those mentioned in the various progressive movements detailed in Part One of this book, that have people putting their faith into action. We can debate the value of the wall separating church and state as as an abstract or utopian concept, but the conservative agenda that claims to be Christian is calling for us to be open about how and why we're fighting for the common good as Christians. And when we do, I argue that the strongest reason for engaging in politics explicitly as a progressive Christian is the rise in Christian nationalism and overt theocratic appeals we're seeing today.

"Politics Is Divisive and Doesn't Belong in Church"

Let's look at the inverse of the first objection. Progressive Christians value inclusion. But this, like the separation of church and state, can also be taken too far. Some people are scared that mixing religion and politics will make conservatives feel unwelcome in their churches. No matter what someone has done or believed, everyone is invited into the redemptive work of following Jesus.

This is the radical welcome of Jesus. It is not a radical welcome to come into the movement and object to the values and shift priorities away from social justice. The foundational question for us is, "What would Jesus do?" and not, "What will the most moderate person in the congregation tolerate?" That's not inclusion; it's a hostage situation.

Division is a fact of life. As the son of two labor union organizers, I've seen "division" among workers demanding their rights in the workplace and their bosses calling the organizing drives "divisive" my entire life. Yes, this "division" was sometimes very painful when the negotiations broke down and workers had to go on strike. But the division reflected a natural tension between the workers and the people at the top trying to profit inequitably off the labor of the people at the bottom. That type of conflict and division has led to advances in workplace protections, like the forty-hour workweek and child labor laws. So, it's not the worst kind of division.

Every one of the bold advances in our society led by progressives has been labeled "divisive"—often as a way to hinder the work. And we need to be clear that the actions needed to reclaim progressive Christianity in the public square will be labeled "divisive." Wresting control from conservative Christianity for what it means to be "Christian" in the United States today won't happen without a fight. Fights are divisive by nature.

> We need to be clear that the actions needed to reclaim progressive Christianity in the public square will be labeled "divisive."

But we should always keep in mind that Jesus was the cause of division in his own time. Jesus's ministry and teaching were extremely divisive, challenging the status quo and upsetting those in power. So much so, the Gospels tell us, that the religious and political leaders of his time conspired to put him to death. Many of Jesus's followers were put to death for following this radical way of love. In the Gospel of Luke 12:49–53, we see some of Jesus's harshest language in the Gospels:

I came to bring fire to the earth, and how I wish it were already kindled! I have a baptism with which to be baptized, and what stress I am under until it is completed! Do you think that I have come to bring peace to the earth? No, I tell you, but rather division! From now on five in one household will be divided, three against two and two against three; they will be divided:

father against son
    and son against father,
mother against daughter
    and daughter against mother,
mother-in-law against her daughter-in-law
    and daughter-in-law against mother-in-law.

This passage sounds harsh coming from Jesus, who talked about loving your neighbor (even your enemy), turning the other cheek, welcoming the prodigal son home, and healing and comforting the afflicted. This passage can sound harsh, too, in our current political environment that is rife with politicians and media outlets that intentionally divide Americans by race, religion, sexual orientation, and any other division they can identify for political benefit—and that have exposed deep divisions in our country that we so strongly desire to see healed. We crave a time of no division, because we are surrounded by so much of it. The thought of more division is exhausting.

But this isn't the only time Jesus speaks about division. In her book *Holy Disunity*, Rev. Layton Williams discusses another passage: "Jesus doesn't bring about the end of separation. In fact, he charges his followers to set themselves apart from the world. In the Gospels of both Matthew and Mark, he comes upon fishermen—first Simon (called Peter) and his brother Andrew, and then James and John, the sons of thunder (best descriptor ever, by the way). And in both tellings of the story, the text says that Jesus walks up to these guys who are making their living and commands them to drop their nets and follow him (Matt 4:18–22; Mark 1:16–20). And they do! Right then and there, they abandon their nets, their livelihood, and their communities, and they follow Jesus . . . Separation is not only present in Christ's ministry and in his call to faithfulness, it's crucial."[106]

Jesus was the cause of division in the most sacred unit of society: the family. In any given family, only some of the family members got it. Thus father was turned against son, because only the son followed Jesus's commandment by loving God and loving neighbor as himself. Everyone didn't drop what they were doing like the first disciples, leave behind their fishing careers, and start believing in radical community, where the first shall be last. If Jesus even caused division among families, you know he causes division among communities of worshippers and in society in general. The act of overturning tables in the temple was not an act of appeasing everyone. The Acts of the Apostles is the story of the early Christ movement catching fire, but it's certainly not the story of the movement catching fire with everyone.

Try it. The "Politics of Love Thy Neighbor" agenda outlined in chapter 14 will undoubtedly be seen as "divisive" if you stand up in a church and pronounce it as divinely sanctioned tomorrow—even though we believe it is. It will be labeled "divisive" because those who profit from the fear and inequality of our present political and economic systems; those who actively seek out more and more of the temptations of wealth, status, and power; and those who rule now aren't just going to give it all up and follow Jesus.

People in power aren't going to sit idly by and watch us radically reorient the economy so that we measure our economic health by how the people at the bottom are doing. Hypocritical religious leaders aren't going to abandon their pulpits when we call them out as charlatans in favor of religious leaders who actually practice what they preach, who are the true servant leaders. The billions and billions of dollars in the military-industrial complex mean there are many people whose entire livelihood is invested in keeping militarism going. An end to the cycle of violence where you hit me, I hit you, and we go on for generations—a cycle of violence that continues today with weapons that could destroy the earth many times over—means an end to their way of life. We can't expect them all to drop everything and follow Jesus.

Religious and political leaders—just like in Jesus's own time—are going to resist this coming Reign of God for it spells an end to what they know and love. How we follow Jesus and the Way of Life brings division, even within families and most definitely within communities.

Luke 12:49–53 isn't about Jesus's desire for division, but a simple statement that division will be part of the cleansing fire.

Everybody is invited into this work of redemptive love and revolution of values in our society. Not one person, no matter where they fall on any divisive issue, is ever shut out of God's love or denied their dignity as somebody made in the image of God. When Jesus says in Luke 14:26, "Whoever comes to me and does not hate father and mother, wife and children, brothers and sisters, yes, and even life itself, cannot be my disciple," he asks people to make the radical choice of following him and the mission of turning society upside down by liberating the oppressed. The focus is on the people turning away from all parts of life that keep them back from following the Way of Life.

The focus here is not on a desired exclusion of family or friends or people we consider "on the other side"; it's on keeping us committed to the cause of justice and peace even when some people refuse to join us. Separation isn't easy, but it's inevitable. The foundation of being able to live with this separation is that our intention and desire are wholeness. We just aren't always going to find it. But we should never stop hoping for that wholeness, for the new heaven and new earth we read about in Revelation.

As we take up the holy, yet sadly divisive, cause of immigrant rights, may we always hold out hope for the ICE agent to start dismantling the cages herself. As we take up the holy, yet sadly divisive, cause of economic dignity, may we always hold out hope for the bankers to declare a Year of Jubilee when all debts will be forgiven. As we take up the holy, yet sadly divisive, cause of LGBTQ rights, may we always hold out hope for our family members who stand on the side of division to see the light of God's equality and join us on the side of love.

Division gets a bad name when it's set against what we desire, like when we seek to turn one of our friends against another friend because it makes us feel better. Or when we resist addressing our own internal emotional issues and instead act out against our neighbors. This is the kind of division we are seeing coming from Washington politics and the media.

But we shouldn't let that un-Christlike divisiveness give all division a bad name. Christ calls us to be divisive if that means we stand up for immigrants during this frightening time or if that means we speak up for a friend or family member who we feel is being unfairly maligned, or when we bring Christ's holy fire to earth through prophetic social justice work. Not everybody is going to agree with us, and while we lament that reality, we don't let it deter us.

We also have to come to terms with the reality that conservative Christians are not going to pick up their tools of social control and political pressure and go away. They're not going to give up and decide that progressives are correct, even though a lot of activism in the realm of Christianity and politics seems aimed at this goal.

One of the most controversial lines in the Gospels, along with the line about separating families cited earlier in this chapter, is Jesus telling his disciples, "For you always have the poor with you, but you will not always have me" (Matt 26:11). As with the statement about family being divided against family, this isn't an endorsement of the poor staying poor or of the righteousness of that fact, but rather a statement of reality. Because of all the evil we see in society, rooted in valuing money over people, we are going to continue to see economic inequality. Likewise, even though we don't desire to see conservative Christians abuse the Bible and continue the tradition that goes back to the slaveholder version of Christianity, it's a reality.

There's always been a robust debate—and division—around what it means to follow Jesus. We see that in the early church, as far back as Acts, some people always look to Scripture and a tradition of exclusion to argue for rigidly enforcing their view of what is right. It's up to us not to destroy them or convince them to stop, but to be louder.

"Power Corrupts You"

Among those thirty-five million-plus consistently progressive Christian adults in the United States, a small but dedicated number have run for elected office. John Lewis is one example of someone who doesn't shy away from talking about how his faith and progressive politics go hand in hand. As a young Baptist minister, Lewis was the youngest speaker at the March on Washington in 1963. His rhetoric at the speech sounds a lot like the progressive Christian clergy I hear speak today.

"My friends, let us not forget that we are involved in a serious social revolution," Lewis declared. "By and large, politicians who build their career on immoral compromise and allow themselves an open forum of political, economic and social exploitation dominate American politics."[107]

Lewis indicted the racism prevalent in both the Republican and Democratic parties then: "There are exceptions, of course," he added. "We salute those" and he went on to name names of the Republicans and Democrats who were not advancing civil rights legislation.

"But what political leader can stand up and say, 'My party is a party of principles'? Where is the political party that will make it unnecessary to march on Washington? . . .

"We do not want to go to jail, but we will go to jail if this is the price we must pay for love, brotherhood and true peace. I appeal to all of you to get into this great revolution that is sweeping this nation. Get in and stay in the streets of every city, every village and hamlet of this nation until true freedom comes, until a revolution is complete. We must get in this revolution and complete the revolution."

The career of Lewis has been defined by his catch phrase "good trouble," of protesting, getting arrested, and generally calling the country to live up to its purported values of liberty and justice for all. This "good trouble" of prophetic critique is something progressive Christians and especially progressive Christian clergy are good at doing. By our very nature, progressives are anti-authority, and critique of those in power—of all political parties—comes naturally.

During President Obama's administration, progressive faith leaders joined immigrant rights activists to hold him accountable for three million deportations he oversaw as president. This was done in the great tradition of not giving a "pass" to people who are part of our own tribe and actually holding our own leaders to a higher standard.

But as much as we need "good trouble," we also need "good power." And John Lewis is someone who has been involved in wielding "good power." He got elected to the US House of Representatives and has lived out his values as one of the politicians who tries to actually legislate the "serious social revolution" he talks about as an ordained minister and activist.

Building power—not authoritarian power, but grassroots, people power—by mobilizing voters and organizing infrastructure is how the values we care about concerning social and economic justice come about in our society. The labor movement doesn't critique powerful corporations and ask them to do the right thing; they build power for workers by organizing. Does building that power sometimes lead to a few corrupt union leaders? Of course. But that's not proof that the labor movement's power-building for workers' rights doesn't successfully give them a voice. Power-building comes with a certain amount of compromise. The modern political proverb "If you're not at the table, you're on the menu" couldn't be truer for people who would rather be yelling at the table from afar.

> As much as we need "good trouble," we also need "good power."

What does power-building for progressive Christians and the religious left look like? There are many ways to build power, but it generally breaks down to identifying a base of supporters that can be activated for social action. My first taste of this work was in college interning for Faith in Public Life in Washington, DC.

"We believe that faith has a critical role to play in shaping public policies and influencing decisionmakers," Rev. Jennifer Butler, Faith in Public Life's founder and PC(USA) pastor, told NPR about the rise of the religious left under Trump. "Our moral values speak to the kinds of just laws that we ought to have."[108] Since 2008, they've worked across religious traditions with a focus on clergy and have amassed a "base" of more than 50,000 faith leaders at the time of this book's writing. I've stayed closely connected with their work and see them as one of the most exciting groups unafraid of being boldly progressive.

I've also worked for the past couple of years with Faithful America, an online organizing group. They use the model pioneered by MoveOn to mobilize progressive Christians online. Founded in 2004, Faithful America is the largest online group of Christians taking action for social change, focused on mobilizing people in the pews. With more than 150,000 members, they regularly deliver petitions signed by more than 10,000 Christians. Some Faithful America members may be in churches where the clergyperson is unsupportive of the cause or doesn't feel they can support it publicly without being "divisive." Faithful America harnesses the power of digital technology to build this kind of grassroots support toward targeting campaign victories.

When the evangelical relief organization World Vision announced plans to stop discriminating against gay and lesbian people and then reversed themselves because of pressure from conservative Christians, more than 17,000 Faithful America members successfully called on Google's Director of Corporate Giving to resign from World Vision's board of directors. More than 20,000 Faithful America members called on MSNBC to drop the Family Research Council's Tony Perkins from appearing on air to spread his conservative Christian hate.[109]

After Trump's election, I felt the need to do *something* in addition to writing about the need for all of us to reclaim our faith. So I started my own effort. The resistance to Trump started on the very same weekend as Trump's inauguration with the Women's March. It continued with the Science March, supported the rule of law, which had been undermined through Trump's obstruction of justice in the Mueller Russia investigation, and more. So many progressive Christians were involved in these efforts, but there were few resources for them. That's why I created The Resistance Prays, a daily prayer devotional aimed at spiritually and politically defeating Trumpism. I wanted to help empower activism and deepen it through daily prayer and reflection on a passage of Scripture.

It started as a Facebook post. The response was overwhelmingly positive.

The devotional now reaches more than 10,000 people and continues to grow. The most amazing aspect of creating The Resistance Prays has been the response from a growing number of old and new friends who have joined me to co-create the devotional. We now have a community of more than seventy people who help write, edit, and produce social media content. We've addressed all the major progressive causes that lead us to resist Trumpism, including immigration, health care, racial justice, gun violence prevention, foreign policy, economic dignity, LGBTQ rights, reproductive health, and climate change.

The Resistance Prays also helped create a new media outlet for progressive Christian writers. While conservative Christians pump out media products across TV, radio, and print, there are very few outlets for progressive Christian writers to develop their craft. The quantity of religion-focused content on progressive media outlets like MSNBC pales in comparison to their conservative counterparts like FOX News. Generating more awareness of the progressive Christian word can be accomplished by creating new media outlets focused on progressive Christians that inform, inspire, and activate our community while also impacting the larger media environment.

In addition to media, the missing infrastructure on the Christian left is political organizing. This includes hosting political forums, producing voting guides, and even endorsing candidates. One inspiration is Bend the Arc, a Jewish social justice organization, that recently formed a Political Action Committee (PAC) to endorse candidates. This proposal will surely cause pushback from some readers who don't see the role of religious institutions as endorsing political candidates. While I don't think churches should endorse candidates, I believe that new institutions, inspired by progressive Christian values, should endorse. It's the difference between Bend the Arc and your local Reform synagogue endorsing a mayoral candidate who aligns with progressive Jewish values. Churches have a pastoral role to welcome and nurture all people. Progressive Christian political organizations, inspired by our Christian values, will play a different role and serve as a spiritual/political home for progressive Christians. Creating and growing institutions to build power for progressive Christians—and progressive people of faith in general— requires all of us to do our part, whether that's investing a few dollars a month, sharing petitions, or showing up at marches. It also requires investment from large foundations that fund the progressive movement overall. They don't need to be religious foundations to fund the movement, but they should have similar aims in reimagining and reshaping American politics.

While we're building power, we need to also recognize it's a different kind of power than we've seen wielded in politics by conservative Christians. As we look to the Gospels for inspiration, we see servant leadership built on the example of Jesus, where anyone who wants to be first must be last. As we read in the Gospel of Mark:

> Then they came to Capernaum; and when he was in the house he asked them, "What were you arguing about on the way?" But they were silent, for on the way they had argued with one another who was the greatest. He sat down, called the twelve, and said to them, "Whoever wants to be first must be last of all and servant of all." (Mark 9:33–35)

Progressive Christians don't want to be first for the sake of being first. We want to be first in line for the sake of the kin-dom of heaven that's coming to earth. When we listen to Jesus speak about becoming a servant to all, that's a leadership style rather than a call to not assume any leadership. Servant leadership is humble, inclusive, and quick to confess errors along the way as we strive to improve our organizations and ourselves.

> The path to overcoming the concentration of power in the hands of corporations, the NRA, the religious right, and other anti-Christ interests is *not* to simply hope they go away. The answer is to be inspired by God toward collective political and justice-based action that will restore power to the people.

Some of us see Jesus as an anarchist and prophet who spoke "truth to power," but Jesus can also be seen as the leader of a movement for radical change in his society. He did, after all, lead his disciples in what became a movement that reshaped the course of human history. That's the movement we're still a part of today, which calls for faithful leaders and "good power" to advance our mission in our own time. The path to overcoming the concentration of power in the hands of corporations, the NRA, the religious right, and other anti-Christ interests is *not* to simply hope they go away. The answer is to be inspired by God toward collective political and justice-based action that will restore power to the people.

CHAPTER 12

FACING THE ANTI-RELIGION LEFT
AND THE RELIGIOUS RIGHT

Taking our faith to the public square (with as many of our fellow progressive Christians as we can convince to join us) will inevitably lead to being challenged by both the anti-religion left and the religious right. Militant atheists attack any mention of religion as "foolish," and in turn help the religious right make their case against "secular liberals." Conservative Christians don't want to debate us because that would acknowledge our existence, so they seem content to focus on the decline of mainline Protestant membership in order to write us off. As we approach both types of critics, we should be mindful that each has benefitted from the erasure of progressive Christianity in our public square. The secular left and the religious right love fighting one another, and we are a thorn in each one's side.

The Anti-Religious Left

Best-selling author and atheist philosopher Sam Harris writes:

> The truth is that most of our modern values are antitheti-
> cal to the specific teachings of Judaism, Christianity, and
> Islam. And where we do find these values expressed in our
> holy books, they are almost never best expressed there.
> Moderates seem unwilling to grapple with the fact that
> all scriptures contain an extraordinary amount of stupidity
> and barbarism that can always be rediscovered and made
> holy anew by fundamentalists—and there's no principle of
> moderation internal to the faith that prevents this. These
> fundamentalist readings are, almost by definition, more
> complete and consistent—and, therefore, more honest.[110]

No group gives the religious left a harder time than militant
atheists. They pop up at progressive organizing rallies and other
ostensibly friendly spaces, but actively try to silence people of
faith. While there is certainly common ground to build between
religious and nonreligious activists, progressive people of faith
have to prepare ourselves to deal with those who are expressly
anti-religious.

For Sam Harris and other militant atheists, the *real* motivations of religious extremists are always religious and their
non-extremist co-religionists are just providing cover for the
extremists. For Harris, that goes for all religion: "The problem is
that moderates of all faiths are committed to reinterpreting, or

ignoring outright, the most dangerous and absurd parts of their scripture—and this commitment is precisely what makes them moderates. But it also requires some degree of intellectual dishonesty, because moderates can't acknowledge that their moderation comes from outside the faith."[111]

Harris's is the same argument peddled by fundamentalists of all religions who argue that moderate and progressive people of faith are leaving behind the "true" religion and giving in to the culture. "The doors leading out of the prison of scriptural literalism simply do not open from the inside," Harris continues, writing off the long history of religious people who advocated for change and evolved their traditions from within.

This dangerous rhetoric makes sense coming from Harris, a militant atheist, sometimes referred to as a "New Atheist." He's among a number of New Atheists generally considered one part of the "the left" in America. And they represent some of the loudest people attacking religion and its role in public life today. Like the progressive Christian skeptics from the previous chapter, the anti-religious secular left often feels like an intratribal barrier to progressive Christian public expression.

The anti-religious secular left is much smaller and less of a threat to progressive faith than conservative Christians. But because we generally consider these people who attack progressive Christians to be allies in the movement for social justice, it's a tough subject to talk about because criticizing someone we believe to be a part of our "tribe" risks alienation. However, it's critical to address these threats, because they often are what keep us from speaking up. While those who ridicule any mention of God as "superstitious" and overzealous advocates for the separation of church and state both have points to make, extremists in both camps actively suppress progressive Christian expression. It's difficult to engage with them because we don't write them off as easily as the anti-LGBTQ, hateful religious right. But their criticism and fear of progressive expressions of religion are huge impediments to our making progress.

Let's be clear about our problem with militant atheists. It's a narrow concern related to how especially zealous atheists shoot down any mention of faith in public life—even in progressive Christianity that doesn't hold a belief that atheists will suffer some kind of posthumous divine punishment.

It's important to understand how militant atheists and fundamentalists both benefit from holding each other up as their enemies. Militant atheists confirm all of their beliefs about Christianity by focusing on the anti-science, anti-evolution, anti-everything posture of conservative Christians to fit their narrative that all "God talk" is hogwash. But we know those aren't the only two choices. Both would rather we go away and let them fight it out for the future of belief in America.

So how do we compassionately deal with critiques of our public witness? We have the opportunity to acknowledge the great gift of nonbelievers and others challenging beliefs and how Christianity has benefitted from them. Progressive Christianity welcomes doubt and tough questions about reconciling faith and science. We are a faith of "yes, and" rather than "no, but." We all have our own doubts, uncertainties, and questions about faith. Progressive Christianity doesn't need to adopt a defensive posture to these questions as long as they are well-intentioned and not trolling.

Progressive Christians generally don't believe that following Jesus is about saving souls from eternal punishment by a vengeful God who paid a blood-ransom price by killing God's Son Jesus. We don't fear that believing in the "right" things somehow determines our eternal fate. This is as important to state about dealing with atheists as it is with people of other faiths. We can lock arms with atheists and people of other faiths on many issues of social justice and reform.

But, finally, we need to stand our ground about our commitment to be followers of Jesus. This doesn't mean needing an answer to every question about the nature of God or the Bible; it means confidence in our mission and understanding that many people aren't going to "get it."

Throughout religious history, we see many different examples of people sharing the good news of how God turned society upside down in the Bible. Jesus seems to reserve his greatest judgment for religious leaders he called hypocrites. While preaching the gospel in front of conservative Christians can seem difficult and like prophetic preaching that holds them accountable, being vocal about our faith with the threat or presence of militant atheists can be even more difficult. There's a freedom in speaking truth to power and not being invested in trying to get them to believe the "right things." On the other hand, we don't shrink from their telling us that atheism is the only or best way to live.

Writing Off Progressive Christianity
Because of Church Decline

Conservative Christians prefer not to argue with progressive Christians on the merits of faith related to equality and justice work. Any real discussion of Jesus and and eradicating poverty, saving the environment, valuing immigration, human dignity, or other issue would lead people to choose the progressive option. So instead, conservative Christians write off progressive Christians as part of a dying tradition. Conservatives weaponize "church decline" to make us appear irrelevant, but in reality, the story is much more complicated.

It's true that attendance and membership numbers are in decline and it's the one thing most people have heard about mainline Protestant religion in America in the media. Pundits claim we're becoming more "secular" as a country. We can look at the data—and I self-identify as a data geek, especially religion data—but that doesn't tell the backstory about what's happening with Christianity in America.

Many of us with a profound Christian faith don't want to publicly out ourselves as Christian. We don't affiliate with a conservative Christian movement. We love Jesus, his teachings, and the long history of Christian progressive activists inspired by his ministry, but for us, Christianity today looks very little like the teachings of Jesus.

When we talk about "church decline" we need to be honest about what most people associate with church in the United States today. We can't act as if attendance and membership decline happened in a vacuum where American Christianity was known for living out the love of Jesus in the public square.

People who focus on "decline" often talk about mainline Protestantism. It's the most often repeated claim about religion in America today—and curiously, it most often comes from conservative Christians and the media that buys their talking points. In the conservative Christian narrative, liberal/mainline Protestantism is experiencing membership decline because of its bad theology. Progressive Christians, they claim, have abandoned the "true" meaning of Christianity and its beliefs. Conservative Christians will often claim that their values, their clear beliefs, and the promise of escaping eternal torments is more appealing than progressive Christianity.

Now let's look at those numbers. The Southern Baptist Convention has become the leading force behind conservative Christianity today and is experiencing rapid decline. In just the past ten years, they've lost more than one million members.[112] The conservative Christian churches that are growing are those that actively hide and suppress their conservative theology. You won't hear sermons about non-Christians being punished for eternity, how evolution is fake news, or how LGBTQ people need to suffer through the fake science of conversion therapy. Even if it informs their understanding of Christian faith, those will remain unaddressed in order to bring people "into the fold."

While conservative Christians have little room to throw stones at mainline Protestant membership decline, there's an eerie correlation between the driver of mainline Protestant church decline and the rise of conservative Christianity. As conservative Christianity advanced in our public conscious-ness, we have seen a greater conflation of why people don't want to affiliate with Christianity at all. On the Catholic side of the Christian community in the United States, conservative ascen-dancy and the clergy sex abuse scandals have also contributed to membership declines.

Most people who choose disaffiliation from Christianity aren't becoming atheists or even agnostics—they just do not want to identify as Christians. Pew Research Center surveyed three distinct groups of religiously "unaffiliated" Americans—the grow-ing number of Americans (55.8 million as of 2014) who don't choose to affiliate with any religious tradition when contacted by researchers. The three groups are very different: atheists, agnos-tics, and people who claim to be "nothing in particular." Often when people think of "nones," they assume that equates to being atheist, when in reality, atheists make up the smallest percentage (3.1% of the US population) of the three groups. Agnostics are only slightly higher (4%), and the largest group is the "nothing in particular" group (15.8% of the US population).[113]

The "nothing in particular" group is fascinating because only one in five of them cited "I don't believe in God" as a reason they are unaffiliated; about one in four said, "Religion is irrelevant to me." Roughly half of the "nothing in particular" group said that the religious teachings and the positions churches take on social/ political issues were important factors in their status. Being unaf-filiated is not necessarily a rejection of God or even the values of following Jesus. But it does correlate with a disavowal of religious teachings and a rejection of what "Christian" stands for politically and socially in our public imagination.

Another survey on disaffiliation from the Public Religion Research Institute found that "among Millennials who no longer identify with their childhood religion, nearly one-third say that negative teachings about, or treatment of, gay and lesbian people was either a somewhat important (17%) or very important (14%) factor in their disaffiliation from religion."[114]

While disaffiliation makes sense as good people reject bad religion, other indicators of spiritual health remain constant. The "nones" don't want any part of what's largely become a hateful, fearful cult of US Christianity. From 2007 to 2014, Pew measured a jump of 16% to 23% in Americans choosing to be religiously unaffiliated. Yet in this same time period, belief in God only dipped three percentage points, showing that affiliation and belief are distinct ball games. Importantly, the questions about an experience of spiritual well-being actually spiked during the same period. The number of adults who reported feeling a sense of "spiritual peace and well-being" at least once a week rose 7%, from 52% to 59% during the time period. The number of Americans who say they feel a sense of "wonder about the universe" at least once a week also rose 7%, from 39% to 46% during the time period.[115]

Over a much longer period, between 1968 and 2011, belief in heaven and hell has remained constant. The same percentage of Americans believed in heaven (85%) in 2011 as in 1968, according to Gallup. The number of people who believe in hell has actually grown from 66% to 75% in 2011.[116] "Nones" are not anti-religion; they are anti–religious fundamentalism, which is not the same as anti–religion at-large.

What is the trend line toward Americans engaging less with formal institutions that require their physical presence? Fewer Christians are sitting in the pews each Sunday, and those who attend church attend with less frequency. This trend is not unique to religion as other in-person experiences such as shopping malls close and many educational institutions move more online. Physical church buildings will continue to close. And "church" might look different. What has constituted the "traditional" model of church has actually always been changing. It will continue to change in the digital age as well.

Change is not inherently bad. We must rid ourselves of the fear-based anxiety about membership and attendance decline. Changes in religious practice can actually empower us to better follow Jesus and co-create the kin-dom of God together. For instance, during the COVID-19 pandemic we saw many churches adapted to not being able to meet in-person. With confidence and humility, we must trust God that people will join our movement when we put out the call in creative and innovate ways.

"'For where two or three are gathered in my name, I am there among them,'" Jesus says in Matthew 18:20. Yes, he rallies big crowds at times—but his goal is spreading the mission. As we carry forth the mission, sometimes big crowds are called for, like when we are marching on the White House to stop the US from invading Iraq—but crowds are not the mission itself. We need to separate out the consumerist, capitalist striving for numbers, prestige, and adoration of institutions when carrying out Christ's mission.

Maybe if we are a movement of a few thousand people in each state across the country, we can cause some "good trouble" for God and align ourselves with Jesus for the common good. I welcome a smaller, bolder, more Christlike movement of progressive Christians in the United States.

When churches boldly live out faith and become truly progressive, we change the public perception of what it means to be Christian and challenge conservatives. The last few decades aren't any indication of what the church can become when we truly follow Jesus. When the church lives its mission, get back to me on how the numbers are looking.

CHAPTER 13

SIGNS OF PROGRESSIVE CHRISTIAN REVIVAL

While there is much work to be done to contest the meaning of "Christian" in public, progressive Christians haven't been idle; a lot of our time, energy, and resources have been spent pushing for same-sex marriage within our churches and denominations. That's kept many of us busy for the past *five decades.* To be sure, there has been activism for racial justice, gender equality, justice for migrants, the environment, ethical borders, and many more causes. But the internal church-reform battle over recognizing the dignity of LGBTQ people has taken up time, energy, and media attention in mainline Protestant denominations.

While the past few years have brought a true, albeit hard-earned, revolution of values to the "mainline," the more progressive values have also resulted in conservative-leaning churches leaving denominations. But when historians look back at this era of progressive Christianity, they will record us embracing the future of LGBTQ rights as consistent with Christian teaching. On the record too will be that we finally broke free from the hold of the conservatives who remain in mainline denominations, who spent decades dragging their feet about basic human rights.

Of the major mainline Protestant denominations, the United Church of Christ, the Episcopal Church, the Evangelical Lutheran Church in America (ELCA), the Presbyterian Church (U.S.A.), and the Christian Church (Disciples of Christ) have moved in recent years toward removing from their denominational policies prohibitions of same-sex weddings and openly LGBTQ clergy.

As this book is being written, the United Methodist Church appears headed toward a holy schism, moving progressives/moderates to be the inclusive church they've long fought to be, and allowing conservative Methodists to go their own way. It's widely understood that the majority of American members of the United Methodist Church are for evolving the church's stance in favor of allowing same-sex marriage and ordaining openly LGBTQ people. And many local Baptist congregations, which each decide their own policies on the dignity of LGBTQ people, have evolved as well.

A New Boldness from Mainline Protestants

Across the denominations of mainline Protestantism, there seems to be a new boldness to pursue the work of social justice that is now unencumbered due the departure of conservatives. Conservative Christianity was able to grow and prosper because of an internal homogeneity that gave it a loud, unified voice in the public square. Mainline Protestantism, conversely, was made up of conservatives, moderates, and progressives with branding and public perception issues on the macro level.

The conservatives have broken away from the PC(USA), ELCA, and Episcopal Church, and are on the cusp of leaving the UMC. As CNN reported about the possible breakup of the United Methodist Church in particular, "Both sides seem happier, more focused on their missions and less concerned with internal battles."[117]

Examples of this new boldness are evident in a range of issue areas, including immigration, racism, climate change, foreign policy, sexism, and colonialism. The entire Evangelical Lutheran Church in America became a "sanctuary church body" at its 2019 Churchwide Assembly. Earlier in this book (chapter 5), we looked at how a strong tradition within progressive Christianity has been sanctuary churches committed to Jesus's commandment to welcome the stranger. Now we're seeing entire denominations move in that direction.

"Declaring ourselves a sanctuary church-body is about how we talk about the work we are doing, and historically have done, broadening the language we use to describe that work, and using language that the world understands," wrote Christopher Vergara, who led the push for the action at the ELCA Churchwide Assembly, in The Resistance Prays. "We must not think that we do this work because God is in need [of] help in the work of salvation; we do this work because our neighbor is in need. We must remember we have been claimed, gathered and sent into the world, for the sake of the world at such a time as this, so let us open our doors and get ready to welcome the divine."[118]

As the United Methodist Church moves toward embracing LGBTQ rights, we've seen a new boldness from their public advocacy arm in Washington, DC. Their office sits on prime real estate next door to the US Supreme Court and across the street from the United States Capitol building. They have used their church sign to make provocative statements on gun violence prevention, immigrant rights, women's rights, foreign policy, and LGBTQ rights.

"I was a stranger and you tear gassed me," read one sign after Trump's immigration apparatus tear-gassed migrants at the border.

Progressive Christian leaders were also involved in one of the most dramatic, prophetic actions against the Trump administration as they joined with Jewish, Muslim, and other religious leaders at the US border-crossing near Tijuana. Faith leaders marched across the beach with the waves of the Pacific Ocean hitting their feet as they approached the border wall and the awaiting group of heavily armed border patrol officers. Dozens of arrests were carried out. One powerful photo showed UMC Bishop Minerva Carcaño and other clergy being dragged through the ocean by police in riot gear.

Whole denominations are also addressing the whiteness of their own churches and taking overt stances against white supremacy. Churches are looking back on their own histories in light of race and are repenting, as well as supporting reforms and reparations.

That includes Mount Vernon Place United Methodist Church, a church I had walked by many times when I lived in

Washington, DC. I noticed the rainbow flag on the sign and assumed that like my church, Foundry UMC, it was a liberal Methodist church. But a story about Mount Vernon in *The Washington Post* caught my attention.

Pro-slavery Methodists had split from the main Methodist Episcopal Church in 1844 and formed the Methodist Episcopal Church, South. The pro-slavery denomination decided they needed a "representative church" in Washington, DC. That church, constructed in 1917, is now Mount Vernon United Methodist. The pro-slavery and anti-slavery Methodist churches reunited in 1939, and the church has become liberal. Addressing the sins of the past is an important part of being progressive, because we can't fully turn the page without true repentance and change.

"Our church was part of a denomination in which every bishop was a slaveholder. Lord, forgive us and those who came before us," members of the church said in unison to mark its one-hundredth birthday as a congregation. "We gather in a building constructed as a monument to America's original sin." *Washington Post* religion reporter Julie Zauzmer reported that "young and old, members gathered in a lengthy line to sign a banner saying, 'We repent for our roots in white supremacy.'"[119]

At its 2019 Churchwide Assembly, the ELCA passed a new social statement that included the line "We believe that the Holy Spirit is leading faithful Christians, as well as people of diverse religions and worldviews, into deeper discernment about questions of patriarchy and sexism. In our own exploration of these issues, we seek whenever possible to engage our Christian siblings in mutual discernment and common action, acknowledging our own complicity in patriarchy and sexism."[120]

On the international front, the Presbyterian Church (U.S.A.) has been a leader in movement to support Palestinian rights and has divested its denominational funds from companies supplying equipment for Israel's occupation of Palestinian territory.[121] Mainline Protestant denominations are also embracing environmental concerns. In 2013 the United Church of Christ divested from fossil fuels, as did the Episcopal Church in 2015.[122]

"Episcopalians understand the life of the mind is a gift of God and to deny the best of current knowledge is not using the gifts God has given you," then–Presiding Bishop of the Episcopal Church Katharine Jefferts Schori told *The Guardian* the same year the church divested.[123]

Before entering the priesthood at age forty, Jefferts Schori was an oceanographer. "I really hope to motivate average Episcopalians to see the severity of this issue, the morality of this issue," she told *The Guardian.* "Turning the ship in another direction requires the consolidated efforts of many people who are moving in the same direction." What about climate denialism? "I think it is a very blind position. I think it is a refusal to use the best of human knowledge, which is ultimately a gift of God."

The mainline Protestant embrace of climate science is the perfect encapsulation of how the tradition has evolved over the past hundred years in embracing both science and social action. It takes accepting material reality as truth to care about climate change. We can't just pray for God to intervene and stop sea-level rising. It also requires a commitment to the Social Gospel to see that Christians can be agents of change and hold out hope that change is possible.

These denominations are also going back and addressing the Doctrine of Discovery and treatment of Native Americans in the founding of this country. The Episcopal Church adopted a resolution repudiating the Doctrine of Discovery in 2009.[124] The doctrine "justifies the discovery and domination by European Christians of lands already inhabited by indigenous peoples"[125] and has also been denounced by the United Methodist Church, the United Church of Christ, the Presbyterian Church (U.S.A.), and the Evangelical Lutheran Church in America.

New Public Leaders for This Era of Activism

Beyond policy changes in the denominations, we're also seeing progressive Christian leaders emerge as icons in our culture.

Sadly, one of the most prominent voices passed away tragically during the time this book was being written. Rachel Held Evans left evangelicalism for the Episcopal Church and had become one of the most popular writers about progressive Christianity in the United States. Rachel's Twitter account was one of the few that I checked regularly, just to see what she was thinking each day and to learn from her. Sharing her own personal experiences gave millions of Christians like her a model for following Jesus by leaving oppressive church structures. She gave people frustrated with conservative Christianity a place to land and the words to find a new church home.

Another group that has captured a great deal of media attention are "Nuns on the Bus." In 2012 they traveled the country in support of a moral federal budget. The tour, organized by the Catholic social justice group NETWORK Lobby, was a creative new tactic that they have now recreated several times since the original tour. A group of progressive Christians used the same tactic in 2018 and 2020 with the Vote Common Good bus tour that visited several key swing states.

The most prominent voices in our culture among progressive leaders are Rev. Dr. William Barber II and Rev. Dr. Liz Theoharis. Rather than come up with a new tactic like Nuns on the Bus, they've revived a campaign used by Rev. Dr. King. Progressive Christians have always advocated for addressing systemic policies, and the New Poor People's Campaign has used creative organizing and communications strategies to bring attention to their work. Barber, a Disciples of Christ pastor, and Theoharis, a Presbyterian Church (U.S.A.) pastor, are two exciting, bold new faces of the mainline Protestant denominations.

Another mainline Protestant cultural icon is the Episcopal Church's Presiding Bishop, Michael Curry, who electrified the royal wedding of Prince Harry and Meghan Markle in 2018 at Windsor Castle. His fiery sermon was classic progressive Christianity informed by the black church tradition. I was watching it live on TV and knew from the first sentences out of his mouth—"In the name of our loving, liberating and life-giving God, Father, Son and Holy Spirit"—that we were in store for one of the most amazing sermons to reach such a broad audience.[126]

Curry quoted Rev. Dr. Martin Luther King Jr. in the context of calling for a world where "no child will go to bed hungry," where "the earth will be a sanctuary," and where we "study war no more." This is the radical Social Gospel movement and calls on the bold tradition of progressive Christianity.

The Most Rev. Michael Curry surprised commentators expecting a "traditional" sermon from the Church of England, not its American cousin the Episcopal Church. And Curry's faith in action was also on display. Just a few days after his royal wedding sermon, Curry was back in the United States protesting the Trump regime in front of the White House.

J. Herbert Nelson II, the stated clerk of the Presbyterian Church (U.S.A.), has talked about the denomination "moving from an institutional culture to a movement culture."[127] That's true of the entire mainline Protestant church: They have shed the baggage of fighting over same-sex marriage that lasted decades and are now leading boldly into the future in a movement mentality. The denominations are, of course, still institutions, and institutions are inherently change-averse. But what gives me hope about the future of the American church is the progressive direction in which the largest Methodist, Anglican, Lutheran, Presbyterian, and Congregationalist denominations are headed. Many Catholics, predominantly black denominations, and nondenominational Christians are headed that way as well.

That's not to say denominations have "arrived" or that the perfect Reign of God is here, or that you can find the Beloved Community fully realized in any mainline church in America. We need to continue the work of church reform, but the trajectory of mainline Protestantism is full of vitality.

One Friday afternoon in early 2018 I had an idea while waiting for my then-fiancé to meet me at the movie theatre. I knew many progressive churches existed across the constellation of mainline Protestantism, but I didn't know of any good crowdsourced lists. I put out a call for people to nominate churches using a five-point set of criteria:

- spiritually enriching community
- vibrant worship
- social justice warriors
- fully LGBTQ-inclusive
- actively invite people into Christian identity/belonging

I didn't police what each of these meant; I just put out the call for churches living out the good news and trying to grow the movement. By the time I got out of the movie, dozens of responses had come in. I capped the list at one hundred because of my own limited capacity to manage such a project, and because I wanted to make a point rather than create a database. These churches exist and were excited to be included. Churches in thirty-three states, across all the mainline denominations, poured in. And while no church is perfect, in every major city and every state in the country you can find people doing the work of love.

CHAPTER 14

A POLITICS OF LOVE THY NEIGHBOR

"Teacher, which commandment in the law is the greatest?"
[Jesus] said to him, "'You shall love the Lord your God
with all your heart, and with all your soul, and with all
your mind.' This is the greatest and first commandment.
And a second is like it: 'You shall love your neighbor as
yourself.' On these two commandments hang all the law
and the prophets."

—Matthew 22:36–40

We are commanded as followers of Jesus to love God and love our neighbors. All the law and the prophets, the entire witness of Scripture, hang on these two commandments. So too should our political values hang on an ethic of loving our neighbor. I mentioned it before, but Cornel West's quote is apt and worthy of a repeat mention: "Justice is what love looks like in public."

Compelled to judge ourselves and our nation by how the most vulnerable are treated, we can and must envision what a just society would look like and work every day toward bringing it into existence. One political speech in particular stands out to me: Congresswoman Alexandria Ocasio-Cortez appealing to "a politics of love thy neighbor"[128] while campaigning for Bernie Sanders during the 2020 presidential primary. The "love thy neighbor" ethic in our life today, according to her, means passing Medicare for All, ending police brutality, ending the policy of caging children and their parents, ensuring a living wage, and creating a Green New Deal. In other words, the vision of earth as it is in heaven inspired by the Social Gospel and liberation theology. Ocasio-Cortez has captured the imagination of people across our entire country by casting a bold vision and is one of the best examples of how to weave a faith tradition (and her own Catholic faith) into an inclusive appeal in a way that steers clear of the theocratic tendencies of conservative Christians. Her speech should be a model for progressive Christians advocating in the public square.

A Proactive Agenda Separate from Conservative Christians

Working in progressive politics and communications introduced me to the work of Dr. George Lakoff, author of the 2004 book *Don't Think of an Elephant!* It was influential regarding progressive political campaigning. The title comes from an experiment he conducted in his classes at the University of California,

Berkeley, asking students not to think of an elephant; he discovered that when students were asked to do that, not one was able to avoid thinking about elephants. In his book, thinking about elephants becomes the frame, suggesting that asking people not to do something can reinforce an idea of doing something.

Dr. Lakoff illustrates this point with the infamous line from President Richard Nixon, "I am not a crook." Of course, when someone says they're not a crook, your mind thinks about Nixon being a crook. Lakoff writes that progressives must "recognize what conservatives have done right and where progressives have missed the boat. It is more than just control of the media, though that is far from trivial. What they have done right is to successfully frame the issues from their perspective."[129]

His advice boils down to this: "If you keep their language and their framing and just argue against it, you lose because you are reinforcing their frame."[130]

Progressive Christians are extremely skilled at keeping the language and framing of conservative Christians and arguing against it. When we repeat the language of conservative Christians, we lose the public-discourse battle in the process. Think about how many times you've heard progressive Christians argue, "It's not pro-life to . . ." and then say something about capital punishment, treatment of the poor, gutting the social safety net, attacking immigrants, bombing foreign countries indiscriminately, or torture. The well-intentioned arguments continue to reinforce the anti-abortion, "pro-life" framework that conservative Christians have so successfully embedded in our public imagination. Likewise, theologically, we say we're "unfundamentalist" or that we "don't read the Bible literally." But by centering on a conservative Christian framing, we reinforce it—even if we seek to negate it.

So, what does a proactive and aspirational vision of a radical revolution look like in society? We desperately need a political and theological vision—and language—focused on the God-given dignity of every human being. Christians must advocate for a world where every person's dignity is recognized and we must work together with people of all faiths and of no faith to bring this country and world into being.

No matter what the issue may be, it's not difficult to discern what the bold vision of God's Reign coming to earth will look like today. Take the string of shootings we've seen in recent years: The Las Vegas concert. Pulse Nightclub in Orlando. El Paso. Virginia Tech. Sandy Hook Elementary School. Mother Emanuel A.M.E. Church. Sutherland Springs Baptist Church. Marjory Stoneman Douglas High School. We have a biblical-scale plague of gun violence in the United States—most notably present in these mass shootings, but also present in local communities on a daily basis.

There are two possible responses to a plague. The first is to contain and limit its spread. The second is to eradicate the plague completely. Ask yourself which option the God of liberation of the oppressed would want us to pursue. When you are praying, do you pray for slow, incremental change? Or do you pray for a just world where God's love and peace will reign?

"There is something deeply hypocritical about praying for a problem you are unwilling to resolve," theologian Miroslav Volf told journalist Kirsten Powers.[131] Whenever I hear fundamentalist preachers and Republican legislators talk about "thoughts and prayers" after a tragedy, I wish I could hear their actual prayers. Are they praying for a world with no violence, even though that would entail limiting the so-called "right" to own automatic weapons?

As people of faith, we are called to offer not only "thoughts and prayers," but prayer and action, to be eradicators of violence and injustice, not piecemeal reformers. When Jesus is asked his views on any topic, his answers always sound like a radical vision of the Reign of God coming to earth then and now.

What does that mean for something like police brutality? The incremental, technocratic measures like body cameras and more training are not sufficient for a Christian vision for the Beloved Community. A Christian vision is community policing strategies with no deaths from gun violence. Now, after setting the vision, we can work backwards through initiatives like community violence prevention efforts, reforming our criminal justice system, and ending the incarceration state in America.

Whether from mass shooters or the police, it's irrefutable that we've come to accept such horrific violence in the United States. Some advocates cite other countries where this violence is never seen, such as zero mass shootings in 2019 in nations as diverse as Saudi Arabia, Germany, Australia, and the United Kingdom. As Christians we are always called to reflect the love and justice-seeking nature of Christ. A world without violence is a world better living out God's vision of peace.

Likewise, racial justice isn't half-measures aimed at "racial reconciliation" between white oppressors and the people oppressed
by white people. This faux-justice may sound good, but it's paper-
thin. White people can't love neighbors of color without reckoning
with racism past and present. Racial justice for Christians means
affirmative action in the present for public investments in communities of color, and accountability for the past in the form of
reparations and a truth-and-reconciliation commission for the sin
of American slavery. May every legacy of slavery—whether it's a
statue of a confederate general or the policies outlined by Michelle
Alexander in her book *The New Jim Crow*[132]—fall. Christians are
called to be leaders in the explicitly anti-racist movement.

Concerning work and economics, the vision of the kin-dom
is everybody having their basic needs met in a just society. Policies like a universal basic income are the kind of bold vision
that means nobody is dependent on their employer to have their
basic needs met. While reforms of a minimum wage of $15 per
hour are important, a just economy would go way beyond what is
achievable in the current political climate.

On the environment, the kin-dom looks like carbon neutrality
so we can stop the hugely detrimental effects of climate change.
We talk about mitigating climate change and that's hugely important, but a bold vision would be policies and a society that actively
restore creation. "Not destroying the earth" is the bare minimum
of what could be considered caring for God's creation. Care ide-
ally involves bringing back to full thriving health, not just hospice
care to our environment as it deteriorates.

Perhaps the boldest vision for Christians is an understanding that this bold vision applies to everyone everywhere on earth. No national border limits whom Jesus calls us to be a neighbor to. What that neighborliness looks like might not always be the same, but our circle of concern must encompass all of humanity. From a Christian social ethics perspective the question should never be, "How does this policy impact Americans?" Americans have no preferential option from God. The only preferential option in the Bible is for the poor and vulnerable. We should always ask how policies will impact the most vulnerable here and in all nations on earth.

We could go on through a list of causes that affirm social and economic justice and what that bold gospel vision looks like: Universal health care. Education as a human right, not a privilege. Good schools no matter what your zip code is. The right to form a union. Restorative justice. No human being labeled illegal. Contraception and family planning services free and readily available. This chapter isn't an exhaustive list, but an attempt to describe how progressive Christians should approach a proactive agenda with boldness.

> From a Christian social ethics perspective the question should never be, "How does this policy impact Americans?" Americans have no preferential option from God.

A progressive Christian agenda should be defined by our values of loving our neighbor and seeing the God-given dignity of every person. Loving our neighbor means we work for the collective liberation of all people everywhere and aren't content with having enough for ourselves. Why stop short of everything for everyone? We are the richest nation in the history of humanity—we can radically reorient our economy and government to achieve material gains for everyone.

In the Gospels, Jesus says he has come so we can live abundantly. What does abundant living mean to you? This is not a rhetorical question. What does a just society look like to you as you think about how Jesus calls us to be in the world? We shouldn't limit ourselves to what can be achieved in the current Congress. Once we cast a bold vision, it's up to legislators to achieve what they can in each legislative session, within the boundaries of what is possible. But we need to set the goalposts they are aiming for when they move the ball. The conservative goalposts are clear: roll back every progressive advance in our collective economic and social life so that white, straight, rich men can dominate again. And do this under the false guise of following Jesus.

We've come to accept too many parts of our collective life as normal. Take, for example, the exorbitant spending the US gives to militarism and the Pentagon budget. What does a moral budget look like for the Pentagon? We can't end every war overnight and bring all of our troops home from overseas, but that should be the goal. A revitalized peace movement can end violence on a global scale in our lifetimes. We've grown so addicted to militarism that we can't even imagine what it would look like to have a revolution of peace where a Department of Peace had more funding than the Department of Defense. We need a bold vision for peace that is not dictated to stopping one war or to small cuts to military spending—we must cast a bold plan for peace.

What Rev. Dr. King called the Beloved Community; what Christians call the kin-dom of God; what all progressive people call social and economic justice today—we have the resources to bring about a political and spiritual revolution in our nation if we just harness the political and spiritual will.

I often hear religion described as a moderating force on political views. On the contrary, I feel religion often radicalizes progressives. We believe economic and social justice are divinely backed causes. We believe God wants us to join in this work of collective liberation.

Progressive Christians and the Hope of Resurrection

People often ask me what the difference is between secular progressives and Christian progressives. They suggest there is no practical difference and thus progressive people of faith aren't worth mentioning. Well, yes, there is one difference. Progressive Christians believe in the Gospel hope of Jesus Christ crucified, dead, and alive again. We believe in the radical hope of resurrection. That should make us the most idealistic bunch in the progressive movement. Nothing is impossible. Our boldness is the boldness of resurrection people who defy the logic of empire. We can't claim to believe in the resurrection and then argue that we are limited in bringing about the Reign of God—the harmony and peace of all people—in our own time. Progressives of other religions bring their own unique views.

The Sermon on the Mount constitutes a radical reordering of society according to God's priorities. Jesus bestows his blessings upon all the people who occupy lower status in terms of how society views the world:

> Blessed are the poor in spirit, for theirs is the kingdom of heaven. Blessed are those who mourn, for they will be comforted. Blessed are the meek, for they will inherit the earth. Blessed are those who hunger and thirst for righteousness, for they will be filled. Blessed are the merciful, for they will receive mercy. Blessed are the pure in heart, for they will see God. Blessed are the peacemakers, for they will be called children of God. Blessed are those who are persecuted for righteousness' sake, for theirs is the kingdom of heaven. (Matt 5:3–10)

The Beatitudes reveal the best of what it means to be Christian. Our capitalist and military-obsessed society blesses might, domination, greed, selfishness, and toxic masculinity. The Beatitudes affirm every person where they are and everything that the empire looks down on. The Beatitudes are the biggest reason I feel called to follow Jesus. We can enact a politics of blessing and love in our society that, through collective action, seeks to take the burdens off everyone Jesus has blessed. Blessed is every person on earth, and blessed is every activist who builds support for a world where people can thrive and bless others.

One of the calls to the activism of blessing others is to create a political and social vision of protecting the most vulnerable. Among them are children. While starting a family isn't everyone's choice, it's a beautiful decision for those who do opt for it. It's incumbent on all of us to create a society that blesses children and the families surrounding them.

> We can enact a politics of blessing and love in our society that, through collective action, seeks to take the burdens off everyone Jesus has blessed.

That conservative Christians are known as the party of "family values" is a form of gaslighting, when the same group attacks LGBTQ families, attacks the social safety net that supports people, and does all they can to prevent positive pro-family policies. That progressives rarely talk about families is extremely disappointing. Ensuring that *all* families have the support they need to thrive should be of paramount concern to progressives and is part of enacting a politics of blessing. This includes policies like universal childcare, family leave, support for adopting children, free family planning services, and free birth control so families can choose to have children when they're ready.

The greatest hope for our lives is that they may be a blessing to others and that way always be guided by the radical spirit of the resurrection. The vision of a just society that we are called by God to build follows in the long tradition of Harry Emerson Fosdick and Dorothy Day and Rev. Dr. Martin Luther King Jr. We draw inspiration from the followers of Jesus who went before us, look up to role models in our world today like Rep. John Lewis and Rep. Alexandria Ocasio-Cortez, and stand shoulder to shoulder with people of other faiths and of no faith who share common values.

The commandment is to love God and our neighbors. We put that into action by co-creating a just society with God. So too, Jesus commissions all of us to this work of love and justice. Filled with the hope of resurrection and trusting the Spirit to direct us toward a just faith, progressive Christians can and must reclaim our tradition in the public square.

The tradition of boldness that inspired the Social Gospel movement, civil rights movement, peace movement, immigrant rights movement, liberation theology, and so much more continues to move in the hearts and activism of so many progressive Christians today. We are not alone in our concern for social and economic justice. There are millions of other progressive Christians around the country with whom we can link arms and fight together. In fact, the number of consistently progressive Christians is far greater that the number of consistently conservative Christians. The false prophets of the religious right have been exposed with the Trump era, and signs of progressive Christian revival surround us. Let us not only be hearers of the Word, but doers of the Word—and users of words when necessary to contest the meaning of "Christian" in public. May our confidence for a world where everyone has everything they need to live abundantly always be rooted in the life and teachings of Jesus Christ, who continues to guide our movement of love.

ACKNOWLEDGMENTS

While this book is dedicated to my grandmother Frances Bell Graves, because she embodied what it means to follow Jesus and pursue personal and social holiness, it could have easily been dedicated to any member of my family. My sister, Emma Graves Fitzsimmons, who is a reporter at *The New York Times*, has edited many of my published pieces of writing and serves as a role model for me in every way I can imagine. My parents, Judy Graves and Orell Fitzsimmons, instilled the values of social and economic justice in me from birth. They both retired recently from careers (forty-one and thirty-five years, respectively) organizing low- and moderate-income people in community organizations and labor unions. Joining them on the picket line, at marches, and folding leaflets at the union office after school shaped my own beliefs that all people deserve economic dignity.

My husband, John Russell Stanger, is both a source of great personal comfort to me and my foremost thought partner in developing the content of this book. As a pastor, therapist, and former nonprofit executive, John Russell provided feedback at every stage of the publishing process and talked me down from the imposter syndrome that arose at times.

My agent, Giles Anderson, took a chance on me after a cold email with an idea for a book from a first-time author. His guidance made what initially seemed like a daunting process go smoothly. The team at Broadleaf Books has been a pleasure to work with from beginning to end. My editor, Lil Copan, publishing director Andrew DeYoung, and the rest of their team brought this book to life. I'm also grateful to my church community at Highland Baptist Church in Louisville and indebted to my Bible study group at church who reviewed early drafts of this book: Robert Kahne, Kelsey Grizzle, Erin Phelps, Charlie Suer, and Jennifer Neyhart. A number of friends have helped this project along the way, and Amanda Pelletier deserves special recognition for explaining the book publishing process when I first had the idea for a book.

My team of co-creators at The Resistance Prays also deserves recognition. While there are far too many contributors to name each one, I will single out my fellow board members Rev. Amanda Hambrick Ashcraft and Chett Pritchett, as well as Managing Editor Sara Holliday and Washington Editor Katie Adams.

And, finally, I want to thank Twitter. I found my voice online and claimed a space for myself as an openly gay Christian when there seemed to be none for me in established spaces. I've enjoyed "meeting" many new people online, some of whom have turned into real-life friends.

NOTES

1. Albert Mohler, "The Evangelicals: A Conversation with Author Frances FitzGerald," *Albert Mohler Blog*, May 8, 2017, https://tinyurl.com/skpszep.
2. Harry Emerson Fosdick, *The Living of These Days* (New York: Harper, 1956), 52.
3. Harry Emerson Fosdick, "Shall the Fundamentalists Win?" *Christian Work* 102, June 10, 1922.
4. Fosdick, *The Living of These Days*, 148.
5. Fosdick, "Shall the Fundamentalists Win?"
6. Fosdick, "Shall the Fundamentalists Win?"
7. Fosdick, "Shall the Fundamentalists Win?"
8. Fosdick, "Shall the Fundamentalists Win?"
9. Nicholas Kristof, "Reverend, You Say the Virgin Birth Is 'a Bizarre Claim'?" *New York Times*, April 20, 2019, https://tinyurl.com/y2bzqnkd.
10. Kristof, "Reverend, You Say . . ."
11. Fosdick, *The Living of These Days*, 66.
12. Harry Emerson Fosdick, "God of Grace and God of Glory," public domain, 1930.
13. MLKP-MBU, Martin Luther King Jr., Papers, 1954–1968, Boston University.
14. Walter Rauschenbusch, *Christianity and Social Crisis* (New York: Hodder & Stoughton, 1907), 65.

15. Rauschenbusch, *Christianity and Social Crisis*, 46.

16. Brandon Rottinghaus and Justin Vaugh, "How Does Trump Stack Up against the Best—and Worst—Presidents?" *New York Times*, February 19, 2018, https://tinyurl.com/y8wt7326.

17. John F. Woolverton, and James D. Bratt, *A Christian and a Democrat: A Religious Biography of Franklin D. Roosevelt* (Grand Rapids, MI: Eerdmans, 2019), 32.

18. Woolverton and Bratt, *A Christian and a Democrat*, 6.

19. Woolverton and Bratt, *A Christian and a Democrat*, 1.

20. Frances Perkins, *The Roosevelt I Knew* (New York: Viking, 1946), 191.

21. June Hopkins, *Harry Hopkins: Sudden Hero, Brash Reformer* (New York: St. Martin's, 1999), 17.

22. Woolverton and Bratt, *A Christian and a Democrat*, 96–98.

23. Alexandria Ocasio-Cortez, "Alexandria Ocasio-Cortez on her Catholic Faith and the Urgency of Criminal Justice Reform," *America*, June 27, 2018, https://tinyurl.com/ybgyd2n9.

24. Brendan Cole, "Sarah Huckabee Sanders Dismisses Ocasio-Cortez Climate Warning: We'll Leave It to 'Much, Much Higher Authority,'" *Newsweek*, January 23, 2019, https://tinyurl.com/ydffluel.

25. Alexandria Ocasio-Cortez (@AOC), "'Genesis 1: God looked on the world & called it good not once, not twice, but seven times. Genesis 2: God commands all people to "serve and protect" creation. Leviticus: God mandates that not only the people, but the land that sustains them, shall be respected.'" Twitter, January 23, 2019, 5:21 p.m, https://tinyurl.com/qjwyzka.

26. Lauren Markoe, "Bill McKibben Talks Faith on His Way to the Climate March," Religion News Service, April 28, 2017, https://tinyurl.com/yx6tr4z9.

27. Alessandro Gisotti, "Al Gore: Pope Francis a 'moral force' for solving climate crisis," Vatican News, July 4, 2018, https://tinyurl.com/ycy5a3q4.

28. Katherine Hayhoe, "I'm a Climate Scientist Who Believes in God. Hear Me Out," *New York Times*, October 31, 2019, https://tinyurl .com/y4fqw6jf.

29. Daniel Cox and Robert Jones, "The 2016 Religion Vote," Public Religion Research Institute, October 27, 2016, https://tinyurl .com/vx4xc3c.

30. T. A. Frail, "Meet the 100 Most Significant Americans of All Time," *Smithsonian Magazine*, November 17, 2014, https://tinyurl.com /y7u876ve.

31. Gary Dorrien, "Martin Luther King Jr. and the black social gospel," *Faith & Leadership*, June 12, 2018, https://tinyurl.com/ughqtzm

32. Dorrien, "Martin Luther King Jr."

33. Dorrien, "Martin Luther King Jr."

34. Martin Luther King Jr., "Letter from a Birmingham Jail," April 16, 1963, African Studies Center at the University of Pennsylvania, https://tinyurl.com/ovcktqb.

35. King, "Letter from a Birmingham Jail."

36. Randall Balmer, "The Real Origins of the Religious Right," *POLIT-ICO*, May 27, 2014, https://tinyurl.com/y4mxxk6l.

37. Martin Luther King Jr., "Beyond Vietnam," April 4, 1967, MLKEC, INP, Martin Luther King, Jr. Estate Collection, In Private Hands, NYC-7A & 7B, https://tinyurl.com/yyqkbqcy.

38. Michael Long, "Coretta's Big Dream: Coretta Scott King on Gay Rights," *Huffington Post*, January 1, 2013, https://tinyurl.com/r3sjz5q.

39. Long, "Coretta's Big Dream."

40. Long, "Coretta's Big Dream."

41. Gillian Brockell, "'To India I Come as a Pilgrim': Martin Luther King Jr.'s Remarkable Trip To Honor His Hero," *Washington Post*, January 20, 2020, https://tinyurl.com/tp5cmkd.

42. Martin Luther King, Jr., "My Pilgrimage to Nonviolence," *Fellowship* 24, (September 1, 1958): 4–9, https://tinyurl.com/ur7pu52.

43. King, "Beyond Vietnam."

44. King, "Beyond Vietnam."

45. Mitchell Hall, *Because of Their Faith: CALCAV and Religious Opposition to the Vietnam War* (New York: Columbia University Press, 1990).

46. Chris Hedges, "Daniel Berrigan: Forty Years After Catonsville." *The Nation*, May 20, 2008, https://tinyurl.com/txnu2rf.

47. Daniel Lewis, "Philip Berrigan, Former Priest and Peace Advocate in the Vietnam War Era, Dies at 79." *New York Times*, December 8, 2002, https://tinyurl.com/tqr92yx.

48. Hedges, "Daniel Berrigan."

49. Hedges, "Daniel Berrigan."

50. William Sloane Coffin Jr., *Credo* (Louisville, KY: Westminster John Knox, 2004), 9.

51. Coffin, *Credo*, 23.

52. Sharon A. Brown Christopher, "Letter to President Bush," Baltimore-Washington Conference of the United Methodist Church, February 6, 2003, https://tinyurl.com/svorwe2.

53. John Paul II, Letter, *Commonweal Magazine*, https://tinyurl.com /y8pho93a.

54. Cornel West, Twitter post: (@CornelWest), "Justice is what LOVE looks like in public," February 14, 2017. 11:15 p.m. https://tinyurl .com/sxnf83h.

55. Religion News Service, "Religious Groups Issue Statements on War with Iraq," Pew Research Center, March 19, 2003, https:// tinyurl.com/vpslb73.

56. Samantha Power, *A Problem from Hell: America and the Age of Genocide* (New York: Basic, 2002).

57. Unpublished by the author with: Frances Graves. Houston, Texas. 2004.

58. Frances Graves interview.

59. Judith McDaniel, "The Sanctuary Movement, Then and Now," *Religion & Politics*, February 21, 2017, https://tinyurl.com/vm752l6.

60. Kaeley McEvoy. "Reviving the Sanctuary Movement." *Sojourners*. October 6, 2014. https://tinyurl.com/rpx5b8z.

61. Talal Ansari, "Some Churches Offer Refuge from Deportation with 'Sacred Resisting,'" *Wall Street Journal,* August 3, 2019, https://tinyurl.com/vuuo98q.

62. Bobby Allyn and Michel Marizco, "Jury Acquits Aid Worker Accused of Helping Border-Crossing Migrants in Arizona," NPR, November 21, 2019, https://tinyurl.com/scyotww.

63. "Church of the Holy Apostles," 2017 NYC LGBT Historic Sites Project, https://tinyurl.com/yx2cnno9.

64. Heather White, "Five Churches That Stood Up for LGBT People before Stonewall," Auburn Seminary Voices, https://tinyurl.com /rtznrke.

65. Howard Moody and Arlene Carmen, *Abortion Counseling and Social Change* (New York: Judson, 1973), 112.

66. Bridgette Dunlap, "How Clergy Set the Standard for Abortion Care," *The Atlantic,* May 29, 2016, https://tinyurl.com/kvuanyc.

67. Jonathan Dudley, "My Take: When Evangelicals Were Pro-Choice," CNN, October 30, 2012, https://tinyurl.com/u2x4afy.

68. Guthrie Graves-Fitzsimmons, "Life after 'Roe': Clergy Consider Handing Out Morning-After Pill in Church," *Religion Dispatches,* July 10, 2018, https://tinyurl.com/shckd8s.

69. Jordan Teicher, "Why Is Vatican II So Important?" *National Public Radio,* October 10, 2012, https://tinyurl.com/y8qmeobo.

70. Gustavo Gutiérrez, *Liberation Theology: A Documentary History,* trans. Alfred Hennelly (Maryknoll, NY: Orbis Books, 1990), 63.

71. Gustavo Gutiérrez, *The Power of the Poor in History* (Eugene, OR: Wipf & Stock, 2004), 44–45.

72. Larry Rohter, "As Pope Heads to Brazil, a Rival Theology Persists," *New York Times,* May 7, 2007, https://tinyurl.com/rz946ka.

73. Rohter, "As Pope Heads to Brazil."

74. Jim Yardley and Simon Romero, "Pope's Focus on Poor Revives Scorned Theology," *New York Times,* May 23, 2015, https://tinyurl. com/y9q7bxkz.

75. Gustavo Gutiérrez, *A Theology of Liberation* (Maryknoll, NY: Orbis Books, 1973), 13.

76. Gutiérrez, *A Theology of Liberation*, 13.

77. James Cone, *Black Theology and Black Power* (New York: Seabury, 1969), 40.

78. Brittney Cooper, "Black, Queer, Feminist, Erased from History: Meet the Most Important Legal Scholar You've Likely Never Heard Of," *Salon*, February 18, 2015, https://tinyurl.com/tmkdurh.

79. Cooper, "Black, Queer, Feminist, Erased."

80. Bart Gingerich, "Radical James Cone Touts 'Queer People' to UM's at General Conference," Juicy Ecumenism, May 1, 2012, https://tinyurl.com/u9thhyn.

81. Paul Djupe and Ryan Burge, "The Religious Left Is Small but Loud," *Religion in Public Life Blog,* January 8, 2020, https://tinyurl.com/v3uxoqc.

82. Population Division, US Census Bureau. Data presented for 2010 through 2018 are Vintage 2018 population estimates. Each year the US Census Bureau revises their post-2010 estimates. https://tinyurl.com/yxbxaqeo.

83. "The Jesus Movement," The Episcopal Church, https://tinyurl.com/qnf4p2v.

84. David Bebbington, *Evangelicalism in Modern Britain: A History from the 1730s to the 1930s* (London: Unwin Hyman, 1989), 2–17.

85. Guthrie Graves-Fitzsimmons, "Roy Moore Isn't the Only Christian Running for Senate in Alabama," *Washington Post*, December 11, 2017, https://tinyurl.com/ya6q442j.

86. MJ Lee, "God and the Don," *CNN*, June 2017, https://tinyurl.com/uvno5dw.

87. Lee, "God and the Don."

88. Lee, "God and the Don."

89. Daniel Cox and Robert Jones, "America's Changing Religious Identity," Public Religion Research Institute, https://tinyurl.com/yd5lnt6e.

90. Sarah Pulliam Bailey, "'I Am the Chosen One': Trump Again Plays on Messianic Claims As He Embraces 'King of Israel' Title," *Washington Post,* August 21, 2019, https://tinyurl.com/uq4p98o.

91. "Transcript: Donald Trump's Taped Comments about Women," *New York Times,* October 8, 2016. https://tinyurl.com/wd7b7vp.

92. "Transcript of Interview with Senator Clinton," *New York Times,* July 6, 2017, https://tinyurl.com/unvt3qg.

93. Hillary Rodham Clinton, *Living History* (New York: Simon & Schuster, 2003), 23.

94. Emma Green, "Hillary Clinton Wants to Preach," *The Atlantic,* August 6, 2017, https://tinyurl.com/ycncyu3e.

95. "Hillary Clinton speaks on faith, 2016 election," *CNN,* September 7, 2017, https://tinyurl.com/ujzr2bj.

96. Ana Marie Cox, "Why I'm Coming Out As a Christian," *The Daily Beast,* May 30, 2019, https://tinyurl.com/ujflmyz.

97. Cox, "Why I'm Coming Out As a Christian."

98. Sarah Pulliam Bailey, "Evangelicals Helped Get Trump into the White House. Pete Buttigieg Believes the Religious Left Will Get Him Out," *Washington Post,* March 29, 2019, https://tinyurl.com /yxcdz35u.

99. Kirsten Powers, "Mayor Pete Buttigieg's countercultural approach to Christianity is what America needs now," *USA TODAY,* April 3, 2019, https://tinyurl.com/y2pe32x3.

100. The Constitution of the United States," Article VI and Amendment 1.

101. "A Knock at Midnight," Sermon at Mt. Zion Baptist Church in Cincinnati, June 5, 1963, https://tinyurl.com/uaj7awz.

102. Michelle Goldberg, *Kingdom Coming: The Rise of Christian Nationalism* (New York: W. W. Norton, 2007), 6.

103. Michelle Goldberg, "What Is Christian Nationalism?" *Huffington Post,* May 14, 2006, https://tinyurl.com/yx48f5bz.

104. Katherine Stewart, "A Christian Nationalist Blitz," *New York Times,* May 26, 2018, https://tinyurl.com/y88ryh8u.

105. "Christians Against Christian Nationalism," https://tinyurl.com/trsh7ku.

106. Layton Williams, *Holy Disunity: How What Separates Us Can Save Us* (Louisville, KY: Westminster John Knox, 2019).

107. Lauren Feeney, "Two Versions of John Lewis' Speech," *Bill Moyers & Company*, July 24, 2013, https://tinyurl.com/vpl4g4p.

108. Tom Gjelten, "Provoked by Trump, the Religious Left Is Finding Its Voice," *NPR*, January 24, 2019, https://tinyurl.com/y7z7q49q

109. "About Us," Faithful America, https://tinyurl.com/vowzrrv.

110. Sam Harris and Maajid Nawaz, *Islam and the Future of Tolerance: A Dialogue* (Cambridge, MA: Harvard University Press, 2015), 65.

111. Harris and Nawaz, *Islam and the Future of Tolerance*, 65.

112. Bob Allen, "Southern Baptists Have Lost a Million Members in 10 Years," Baptist News Global, June 9, 2017, https://tinyurl.com/sb6hn45.

113. "Religious Landscape Study," Pew Research Center, https://tinyurl.com/y6ttqm72.

114. Daniel Cox, Juhem Navarro-Rivera, and Robert Jones, "A Shifting Landscape: A Decade of Change in American Attitudes about Same-Sex Marriage and LGBT Issues," Public Religion Research Institute, February 26, 2014, https://tinyurl.com/ycgwvle2.

115. "US Public Becoming Less Religious," Pew Research Study, November 3, 2015, https://tinyurl.com/yyh3lu36.

116. "Religion," Gallup, https://tinyurl.com/y3q7vwjb.

117. Daniel Burke, "The Methodist Church Will Probably Split in Two over Homosexuality, and That's Bad for All of Us," *CNN*, January 17, 2020, https://tinyurl.com/smndrcy.

118. Christopher Vergara, *The Resistance Prays*, August 11, 2019, https://tinyurl.com/uf267ld

119. Julie Zauzmer, "On Its 100th Birthday, a Church Repents For Its Racist Founders," *Washington Post*, October 8, 2017, https://tinyurl.com/qna7tla

120. "Faith, Sexism, and Justice: A Call to Action," Evangelical Lutheran Church in America, https://tinyurl.com/s57rbnp

121. Laurie Goodstein, "Presbyterians Vote to Divest Holdings to Pressure Israel," *New York Times*, June 20, 2014, https://tinyurl.com/yah8b9qc.

122. Emily Atkin, "Episcopal Church Votes to Withdraw Investments in Fossil Fuels," *ThinkProgress*, July 6, 2015, https://tinyurl.com/wtbhwar

123. Suzanne Goldenberg, "Climate Denial Is Immoral, Says Head of US Episcopal Church," *The Guardian,* March 24, 2015, https://tinyurl.com/vgnyrsx

124. Mary Frances Schjonberg, "General Convention Renounces Doctrine of Discovery," Episcopal Church, August 26, 2009, https://tinyurl.com/wl48oqb

125. Emily McFarlan Miller, "Denominations repent for Native American land grabs," Religion News Service, August 22, 2018, https://bit.ly/3fsj3iy.

126. Maquita Peters, "Bishop Michael Curry's Royal Wedding Sermon: Full Text of 'The Power of Love,'" *NPR,* May 20, 2018, https://tinyurl.com/y7mw2c3l

127. Emily McFarlan Miller, "Presbyterians Aim to Revive Mainline Denomination," *Religion News Service,* June 14, 2018, https://tinyurl.com/w8kmgyr

128. "Alexandria Ocasio-Cortez on Love Thy Neighbor Politics," YouTube, https://tinyurl.com/w67wkp4

129. George Lakoff, *Don't Think of an Elephant!: Know Your Values and Frame the Debate: The Essential Guide for Progressives* (White River Junction, VT: Chelsea Green, 2004), 33.

130. Lakoff, *Don't Think of an Elephant!,* 33.

131. Kirsten Powers, "Why 'Thoughts And Prayers' Is Starting to Sound So Profane," *Washington Post,* November 6, 2017, https://tinyurl.com/y7mvaklx

132. Michelle Alexander, *The New Jim Crow: Mass Incarceration in the Age of Colorblindness*, 10th anniv. ed. (New York: New Press, 2020).